New Casebooks

MRS DALLOWAY
and
TO THE LIGHTHOUSE

New Casebooks

New Casebooks

MRS DALLOWAY
and
TO THE LIGHTHOUSE

VIRGINIA WOOLF

EDITED BY SU REID

MACMILLAN

First published 1993 by
MACMILLAN PRESS LTD
Houndmills, Basingstoke, Hampshire RG21 6XS
and London
Companies and representatives
throughout the world

ISBN 0–333–54141–3 hardcover
ISBN 0–333–54142–1 paperback

A catalogue record for this book is available
from the British Library.

10   9   8   7   6   5   4   3
03   02   01   00   99   98   97   96

Printed in Hong Kong

Virginia Woolf: To the Lighthouse: ed. Morris Beja

This title is available in the original *Casebook Series*, offering a
wide range of earlier critical views on the text.

For a full listing of the original *Casebook Series*, please write to
the Customer Services Department, Macmillan Distribution Ltd,
Houndmills, Basingstoke, Hampshire RG21 2XS.

In happy memory of
Margaret and Harry Massey

Contents

Acknowledgements

I am grateful to the Series Editors, Martin Coyle and John Peck, for their patience and very considerable help; to my friends and students at the University of Teesside for their companionship and inspiration; and to my family.

The editor and publishers wish to thank the following for permission to use copyright material:

Elizabeth Abel, excerpts from ' "Cam the Wicked": Woolf's Portrait of the Artist as her Father's Daughter' in Jane Marcus (ed.), *Virginia Woolf and Bloomsbury. A Centenary Celebration* (1987) by permission of Macmillan, London and Basingstoke, and Indiana University Press; Gillian Beer, excerpts from 'Hume, Stephen, and Elegy in *To the Lighthouse*' in her *Arguing With the Past. Essays in Narrative from Woolf to Sidney* (1989), by permission of Routledge; Rachel Bowlby, excerpts from *Virginia Woolf, Feminist Destinations* (1988), by permission of Basil Blackwell Ltd; J. Hillis Miller, excerpt from 'Mrs Dalloway, Repetition as Raising of the Dead' in his *Fiction and Repetition. Seven English Novels* (1982). Copyright © 1982 by J. Hillis Miller, by permission of Basil Blackwell Ltd and Harvard University Press; Margaret Homans, excerpts from *Bearing the Word. Language and Female Experience in Nineteenth-Century Women's Writing* (1986), by permission of The University of Chicago Press; David Lodge, excerpts from *The Modes of Modern Writing. Metaphor, Metonymy, and the Typology of Modern Literature* (1977), by permission of Edward Arnold Publishers; John Mepham, excerpts from 'Figures of Desire: Narration and Fiction in *To the Lighthouse*' in G. Josipovici (ed.), *The Modern English Novel: the Reader, the Writer and the Work* (1976), by permission of Open Books Publishing Ltd; Makiko Minow-Pinkney, excerpt from *Virginia Woolf and the Problem of the Subject*: *Feminine Writing in the Major Novels* (1987). Copyright © 1987 by Makiko Minow-Pickney, by permission of Harvester-Wheatsheaf and Rutgers University Press; Toril Moi, excerpt from 'Introduction: Who's afraid of Virginia Woolf?' in her *Sexual/Textual Politics*: *Feminist Literary Theory* (1985), by permission of Methuen & Co; Jeremey Tambling, excerpts from 'Repression in Mrs Dalloway's London', *Essays in Criticism*, 39 (April, 1989), by permission of Essays in Criticism.

General Editors' Preface

The purpose of this series of New Casebooks is to reveal some of the ways in which contemporary criticism has changed our understanding of commonly studied texts and writers and, indeed, of the nature of criticism itself. Central to the series is a concern with modern critical theory and its effect on current approaches to the study of literature. Each New Casebook editor has been asked to select a sequence of essays which will introduce the reader to the new critical approaches to the text or texts being discussed in the volume and also illuminate the rich interchange between critical theory and critical practice that characterises so much current writing about literature.

In this focus on modern critical thinking New Casebooks aim not only to inform but also to stimulate, with volumes seeking to reflect both the controversy and the excitement of current criticism. Because much of this criticism is difficult and often employs an unfamiliar critical language, editors have been asked to give the reader as much help as they feel is appropriate, but without simplifying the essays or the issues they raise. Again, editors have been asked to supply a list of further reading which will enable readers to follow up issues raised by the essays in the volume.

The project of New Casebooks, then, is to bring together in an illuminating way those critics who best illustrate the ways in which contemporary criticism has established new methods of analysing texts and who have reinvigorated the important debate about how we 'read' literature. The hope is, of course, that New Casebooks will not only open up this debate to a wider audience, but will also encourage students to extend their own ideas, and think afresh about their responses to the texts they are studying.

John Peck and Martin Coyle
University of Wales, Cardiff

Introduction

SU REID

Reviewers of *Mrs Dalloway* and *To the Lighthouse* at the time of their publication,[1] although enthusiastic, were often puzzled.[2] They described the novels as 'poetic' rather than realistic; they found them sometimes difficult to read and their characters and events unclear. Many subsequent readers and critics have agreed. But the more recent critics featured in this book are beginning to see a different Virginia Woolf, a writer whose novels are by no means remote from 'real life', and whose stories are carefully and coherently put together.

During Woolf's lifetime it quickly became an established orthodoxy that she was an 'experimental' novelist whose readers should look for symbols and evocations of mood in her work rather than for sequences of events, for stories. When she died in 1941 friends and critics joined in confirming this idea. In a very hostile article in the journal *Scrutiny*, F. R. Leavis attacked her whole career as one misguidedly directed towards writing about vague experiences in the mind; he thought *To the Lighthouse* was her 'one good novel' because it seemed to be a recognisable representation of her father, the Victorian writer Sir Leslie Stephen.[3] Even her friend E. M. Forster wrote in his memorial lecture that she 'dreams, designs, jokes, invokes, observes details' but perhaps could not 'tell a story or weave a plot' or 'create character'.[4]

Through the decades that followed it became normal for critics to impose complex symbolic meanings onto the novels, and, at the same time, to regard reading them as an often baffling experience without direct relevance to recognisable events. James Naremore's description of the experience of reading Woolf perhaps sums up this view:

1

one sometimes has the impression of being immersed in a constantly
moving liquid, immersed so deeply that the people and things in her
books become muffled and indistinct. . . .[5]

The essays in this book, however, which were all published after
1975, inaugurate new ways of reading the novels. Above all, they
show that their narratives are tightly and logically constructed, that
they relate directly to important historical issues, and that they
combine with Woolf's more polemical essays to say provocative
things about the lives of women.

I

The first three essays, those by David Lodge, John Mepham and
J. Hillis Miller, all discuss the narrative construction of the novels. In
doing so they suggest how readers might work out a clear understanding of the novels' stories for themselves. To an extent, they all
build on the much earlier work of Erich Auerbach who concluded his
long book *Mimesis*[6] with an examination of section 5 of 'The Window', the first Part of *To the Lighthouse*.[7] This is the section of the
novel in which Mrs Ramsay measures against her son James's leg the
stocking she is knitting for the lighthouse-keeper's boy. While she
does this she thinks about the shabbiness of the house and her
responsibilities to her household; and someone else, the voice of the
novel's narrator, wonders why she looks so sad and remembers, in a
parenthesis, an occasion when another character, William Bankes,
thought about her great beauty. Auerbach's essay, 'The Brown Stocking', was reprinted in Morris Beja's original Casebook on *To the
Lighthouse*.[8] In it Auerbach asks, rhetorically, who is speaking during the passage about Mrs Ramsay's appearance of sadness.[9] He
concludes that since it is none of the characters it must be 'the
author': but an 'author' who is something different from Virginia
Woolf, appearing not to have total knowledge of 'his' characters.[10]
Auerbach demonstrates that the voice recounting the events and
arguments throughout the novel is itself a construct, not simply the
knowing presence of the author. More recently it has become a
familiar truth to students and critics that the narrative voice of a text
is indeed something constructed within the language of that text
itself, that it is not simply 'the author'; but Auerbach was the first to
demonstrate the importance of this idea for a reader who wishes to
follow Woolf's novels clearly. Lodge, Mepham and Miller show, in

different ways, how careful attention to the narrative voices of *Mrs Dalloway* and *To the Lighthouse* will lead the reader to a clearer understanding of each of the novels as a whole.

David Lodge's book *The Modes of Modern Writing*[11] attempts to distinguish between 'realist' and 'modernist' writing. Its discussion of Virginia Woolf (essay 1, below) takes her work as an example of 'modernism'. Briefly, Lodge's argument is that the more 'modernist' a text is the greater is its use of metaphor and symbolism; and his account of Woolf sees her novels, each constructed differently from the others, as becoming progressively more reliant on metaphor.

Lodge's idea is that this use of metaphor contrasts with 'realist' narratives, those that appear more obviously to describe real events and places existing outside the text. 'Realist' writing, he argues, displays fewer metaphors in its language and a greater preponderance of metonymy. The useful distinction between metaphor and metonymy, which Mepham also employs in the second essay in this book,[12] is explained simply by Lodge in the earlier chapters of *The Modes of Modern Writing*, and derives from theories about the operation of language itself. In a metaphor words are *substituted* in the text for other possible words which have a point of similarity with them but are most noticeably *different*. In metonymy words *suggest* other words or images in addition to themselves. Lodge demonstrates the distinction in a sequence of short sentences. If 'Ships crossed the sea' were changed to 'Ships ploughed the sea', he writes, then 'ploughed', substituting for 'crossed', would be a metaphor. But if the sentence were changed to 'Keels crossed the deep', then 'keels' and 'deep' would indicate aspects of 'ships' and 'sea' rather than replace them, and the function would be metonymic.[13] The reader of a metaphor has to collude with a process of selection and substitution among words that are importantly *different* in meaning from each other; the reader of metonymy combines words in the text with other possible and perhaps *similar* or contiguous words in his or her mind.

Lodge's application of this idea, in broad chronological terms, to Woolf's novels from *The Voyage Out*[14] to *The Waves*[15] enables him, and his readers, to begin to understand that each of the novels is indeed constructed differently from the others. In particular, *Mrs Dalloway* is seen to be distinct in its invention of a metaphoric procedure: the narrative voice switches from character to character and event to event by repeatedly substituting something relevant but also different for each one.[16] It frequently, for example, substitutes one character for quite a different one when both are simply looking at the same thing – the aeroplane perhaps. By contrast Lodge thinks that *To the Lighthouse* is deliberately less consistent, that it teases readers with sequences of parentheses and of 'figurative expressions' that prevent them from forming a clear image.[17]

But Lodge is in some ways an impatient reader of Woolf. Like many earlier writers he describes the novels as 'essentially plotless',[18] and he assumes all the time that they centre on the representation of an abstract idea. Mepham (essay 2) and Miller (essay 3) each examine the narrative voices of one of the novels in closer detail. They enable us to see that *Mrs Dalloway* and *To the Lighthouse* do have plots, and that they are closer than has been thought to the tradition of the realist novel.

John Mepham's essay is specifically concerned to work out the form of the narration in *To the Lighthouse*. Mepham distinguishes clearly between what he calls the 'fiction' of the novel, the characters and sequence of events that we imagine have happened, and its 'narration', the ways in which we are told about those characters and events, and the connections between the events.[19] He shows that in Part I, 'The Window', the narration follows its own 'subjective' line of thinking, setting this against the 'objective' order of events and the time we imagine them to have taken.[20] In the opening sections, for example, the brief conversation that takes up the present time of the fiction – the conversation from '"Yes, of course, if it's fine tomorrow," said Mrs Ramsay'[21] to '"Perhaps it will be fine tomorrow," she said, smoothing his hair'[22] – represents only a few seconds of imagined time but occupies many pages of the narration's thinking. Mepham also shows that it is indeed the *narration's*, or narrative voice's, line of thinking that it is articulated, not just, as so many critics have supposed, the 'stream of consciousness' of the characters. Any reader of the novel will find it worthwhile to trace carefully the stages by which the narrative voice, throughout 'The Window', moves its own attention from an observation of the characters and their conversation, to a recounting of the silent thoughts of just one of them, and then back again to the conversation in the present time. For example, in the first section Charles Tansley is described as contributing his 'It's due west' to the discussion, and the narrative voice immediately follows Mrs Ramsay's private, unvoiced, reaction into a summary of her children's opinions of Mr Tansley, and her memory of having had to say 'Nonsense' to them, and of trying to curb their hostility.[23] Tansley speaks again – 'There'll be no landing at the Lighthouse tomorrow'[24] – but the narrative voice, having heard and recorded his remark, continues its interest in Mrs Ramsay's thoughts about him, and her memory of having taken him with her into the little town, until it ends its own reverie with the end of the first section. It then returns itself to the present time by means of the very brief second section:

> 'No going to the Lighthouse, James,' he said, as he stood by the window, speaking awkwardly, but trying in deference to Mrs Ramsay to soften his voice into some semblance of geniality at least.
> Odious little man, thought Mrs Ramsay, why go on saying that?[25]

A reader who carefully follows the movement of the narrative voice between the 'present time' of the novel and the various digressions from it, will find that the 'present' consists of a coherent sequence of linked events. The novel opens with the dispute between the Ramsays about the weather and the trip to the lighthouse. While their children and guests pursue their own interests and anxieties, this dispute develops. It turns into Mr Ramsay's outright irritation in section 6, his 'Damn you', followed immediately by his penitent offer to go and ask the coastguards about the weather and Mrs Ramsay's instantaneous acceptance of the power of his opinion.[26] In due course James is taken away to bed and Mrs Ramsay is left to herself, withdrawing from her domestic roles into a few minutes' peace and quiet; but almost immediately she becomes aware that her husband is watching her, and she interrupts her own peaceful time to join him and make him feel, reassuringly, that he is her protector.[27] But the tension between them continues, held at bay during the dinner party by the guests,[28] until it is resolved at the end of the evening, and the end of 'The Window', by another action of Mrs Ramsay's which increases her husband's dependence on her for reassurance. She indicates to her husband that she loves him, not by *saying* so, for he is the one who claims power in speech, but by gesture and by an acknowledgement, justified or not, that he is right about the weather. The two are reconciled, and we are told that Mrs Ramsay had 'triumphed again'.[29] Presumably her triumph consists of knowing that she makes her husband feel comfortable and powerful, at cost to herself and to James.

In essay 2 Mepham draws attention to various examples of the narration's movement from one focus of attention to another in 'The Window', and suggests that 'the transitions are managed . . . "metonymically"'.[30] In different ways the narrative voice moves

from topic to topic by a process of association. This is contrasted by
Mepham with the process at work in Part III, 'The Lighthouse',
where there are two parallel stories, the story of the voyage to the
lighthouse and of the relationships between Cam and James and Mr
Ramsay in the boat, and the story of Lily Briscoe and her painting.
These stories both describe the characters' struggles to stabilise their
memories of Mrs Ramsay, who is now dead. Mepham argues that
the narration, as it switches backwards and forwards between them,
substitutes each for the other in a metaphoric relationship.[31]

Mepham's essay then moves on to define some of the particular
characteristics and interests of the narrative voice of *To the Lighthouse*.[32] It is left to the reader to consider how the narration of 'Time
Passes' compares with that of either of the other two parts of the
novel. But Mepham's discussion does show that *To the Lighthouse* is
both more clearly structured than many critics have realised, and
closer to the familiar tradition of the realist novel which tells a story.
It also accounts very convincingly for the difference many readers
feel between the experience of reading the first part and the experience of reading the third.

Mrs Dalloway, also, can be thought of as close to the tradition of
the realist novel; so J. Hillis Miller argues at the beginning of his
essay (number 3), and Rachel Bowlby puts a similar view (essay 10).
Mrs Dalloway tells how, on the day of the novel, Clarissa Dalloway
relives her decision, made long ago, to marry Richard Dalloway
rather than Peter Walsh.[33] Miller's essay on *Mrs Dalloway*, like
Mepham's on *To the Lighthouse*, is primarily concerned to define
the structure of the narration; and like Mepham's it shows that an
attentive reader can understand the novel's construction, and so see
its story, quite clearly.

Professor Miller's work explores texts in terms of the idea, deriving most immediately from the French writer Jacques Derrida, that
meaning is created during the act of reading: that words do not
straightforwardly represent anything that existed independently of
them. His essay below starts by defining the effect of the traditional
use, in novels, of past-tense verbs by an impersonal narrative voice
who appears to know events in the past and to retell them in the
present; and it describes the familiar but peculiar relationship between the characters and a voyeuristic narrator of this kind.[34] It also
suggests that in *Mrs Dalloway*, unlike most realist novels, the narrative voice has almost no knowledge beyond what the characters
themselves think, but seems to represent a kind of collective con-

sciousness in which the consciousnesses of all the apparently separate characters are involved and are brought back to life.[35] In this way Miller's essay articulates and makes clear to a reader that sense of a fluid relationship between each of the characters which so many critics discussing *Mrs Dalloway* have addressed only vaguely. It shows that all the characters are constructed for us by a single 'mind', and that the apparently chance connections between them of time or place are not random at all but have connections which the reader should pursue. The reader will then perhaps find that the novel's 'story' is actually more than the story of Clarissa's marriage, important though that is. He or she will come to see that *Mrs Dalloway* is a coherent acting-out of how people in London in 1923 – Clarissa, Septimus, Peter, and all the others – are, in different ways, failing to admit and understand the violence and suffering of their past. That past includes domestic repression and sexual tyranny as well as imperial power, and loss and death in the recent war.

The essays by Mepham and Miller, then, rest on different experiences of words and meanings. Mepham's describes how a narrative voice appears to represent past events selectively. Miller's shows how the activity of reading might construct meanings now, in the present moment. But both know that all novels are made with language, not with events or people that exist separately. And they demonstrate by careful attention to the construction of these novels that neither is merely a collection of moments of consciousness, or even of 'poetic' symbols. Both novels clearly dramatise family and public life in the early twentieth century, mainly among the English middle class.

II

The next two essays in this book, those by Jeremy Tambling (number 4), and Gillian Beer (number 5), also show that *Mrs Dalloway* and *To the Lighthouse* are engaged with specific historical circumstance. Tambling defines in detail many of the particular historical and political circumstances in *Mrs Dalloway*, a novel which is set on a single day in June 1923 in a 'real' place, London. Some of these circumstances are explicit in the novel, others are implied. Most obviously they include the First World War of which Septimus is a direct victim, and the British Conservative government of which Richard Dalloway is a member and whose Prime Minister visits Clarissa's party;[36] and London itself in 1923, its sounds and its buildings, some of them then quite new. But Tambling also draws attention to the novel's references to late nineteenth-century socialist movements, to the British Empire and the characters' loyalties to it, and also to the thinking of the time about health and illness and madness, and about sexual identity. In all this, Tambling is doing something very different from Lodge's and Mepham's and Miller's careful examinations of what the novels themselves explicitly say. He is working instead to define the assumptions that form the novel, assumptions we of a later generation can begin to understand and articulate.

Tambling suggests that the central image of Mrs Dalloway is Westminster itself, a series of symbols of desire for power. He argues that this image of domination relates to all the concerns of the novel, including the war, and the possibility of further wars, and the insistent assertions that the war is now over; and to the treatment of Septimus by Holmes and, especially, Bradshaw; and to Clarissa's own anxiety about herself, her health, her choice of husband, her daughter, and her social role. Above all, he argues that the novel shows us a society in which acceptable personal and sexual identities are strictly defined, so that anything other than narrowly conventional heterosexuality becomes subversion or neurosis, and is suppressed.

He does not suggest, however, that the novel is in any sense a polemic against those narrow respectabilities of the period. On the contrary, he argues that it is unable to criticise the society it portrays, except by making some individual characters, especially Bradshaw, dislikeable. In fact, he says, it colludes with the ways of thinking that it also shows to be tyrannical – it colludes, that is, with the definition of personal and sexual distress as medical matters that might be corrected, and with an admiration and nostalgia for imperialist power.

Tambling's essay is clearly very different from the work of many critics in the past who saw Woolf as a trivial writer concerned only with aesthetic sensibilities.[37] In recent years it has become more obvious that her work is engaged with the public events of her day as well as with domestic experience. 'Time Passes', the second part of *To the Lighthouse*, is often now related directly by critics to the First World War,[38] and readers will find it worthwhile to look closely at that novel's accounts of relationships between the social classes before and after the war.

Woolf's novels do not relate to their historical period only by referring to public events, however. Tambling and Beer both show that they engage with philosophical issues of their time. Tambling's account of Westminster as the central image of *Mrs Dalloway* depends upon his perception that the novel's idea of 'character' is what he calls the 'modernist' one.[39] This means that an individual character, or identity, is not seen as fixed, as natural or innate, but as something that is made. It is made progressively through life by the interaction of circumstances – of roles in relation to other people, of places, of prevailing values and judgements. So Septimus, for example, is created by the conflict between his wartime friendship with, and loss of, Evans, and the values he has internalised which demand that he repress suffering. Clarissa is made by her past, her rejected friends, her decision about marriage, and her consequent role as a politician's wife.

Gillian Beer's essay (number 5) reads *To the Lighthouse* primarily as a personal exploration by Virginia Woolf of ideas about individual identity, and the extent to which it is constructed rather than permanent and innate. Beer defines the novel as autobiographical, though not in a naïve way that would simply identify Mr and Mrs Ramsay as pictures of Woolf's own parents. She argues that much of the novel refers directly to the writing of Woolf's father Sir Leslie Stephen,[40] and especially to his discussion of the eighteenth-century philosopher David Hume; and that it works out ways in which Stephen's conclusions about human identity must be both respected and modified.

The main issue, Beer argues, is a debate about whether individuals, and things, exist permanently in themselves and so continue to exist whether anyone is thinking about them or not, or whether that is an illusion and everything exists only as it is perceived. The problem is summed up in Andrew Ramsay's description to Lily of his father's work:

> 'Subject and object and the nature of reality,' Andrew had said. And when she said Heavens, she had no notion what that meant. 'Think of a kitchen table then,' he told her, 'when you're not there.'[41]

A major aspect of the debate, one which Beer sees as central to *To the Lighthouse*, is a series of questions about the identity of the writer or thinker, his reputation and its survival, and his independence of thought or his dependence on humbler men (the examples in the novel are all men). These are issues about which Mr Ramsay is personally anxious.[42]

Beer shows that *To the Lighthouse* follows Stephen's support for the belief that objective existence is an illusion, that perception is really a matter of mental associations put together by circumstances and chance, and that an individual consciousness is therefore neither innate nor fixed nor in any sense permanent.[43] But she goes on to argue that the novel takes these concerns beyond Stephen's ideas, and that in it Woolf keeps the issue alive and develops her own views about human consciousness.

The novel shows its characters longing for permanence, for a belief that individuals do exist and continue to exist as their circumstances change, even that they still exist when dead. But it also shows, especially in 'Time Passes' where things are described when no one is there to observe them, that language itself always creates the illusion of independent 'reality': language can make it *seem* that objects and people exist objectively, and that someone who is not a part of them can watch or know about them, even when there is no such 'someone'. But the novel does not, Beer says, make us choose between the idea that people and things exist essentially and the idea that nothing – not even people – exists except as it is thought about. Instead it allows both its characters and its readers to experience moments of great confidence in the eternal existence and importance of human actions, and almost at the same time to experience a simple acceptance of the transience and insignificance of everything. For example, Lily says 'It is finished' of the end of Mr Ramsay's voyage and his final arrival at the lighthouse – a phrase which even connects his endeavour with the idea of Christ and divine action; and, almost simultaneously, Lily finishes her own painting and the narrative voice calmly reports her simple knowledge of transience, removing all suggestion of grandeur or divinity: 'It was done; it was finished.'[44]

III

Towards the end of her essay Beer refers briefly to the work of the French psychoanalytic philosopher and critic Jacques Lacan.[45] Tambling also refers to Lacan and to another psychoanalyst and philosopher working in Paris, Julia Kristeva.[46] Both references come in the context of suggestions that Woolf's novels dramatise the friction between an authoritarian consciousness asserting permanence – represented by Westminster and by Sir William Bradshaw in *Mrs Dalloway*, and by Mr Ramsay and even perhaps by the operation of language itself in *To the Lighthouse* – and a consciousness of difference and impermanence. Many recent feminist critics see most of Woolf's work as confronting the opposition between assertions of certain knowledge and assertions of difference, of change, of variation. Toril Moi's essay (number 6) proposes that Woolf should be read specifically in this way, and she explains her proposal in terms of a more detailed account of ideas from Lacan and, especially, Kristeva. The essay itself is taken from the opening chapter of Moi's book *Sexual/Textual Politics*[47] which, when it was published in 1985, introduced many readers to these ideas. The overall purpose of the book was to show how Kristeva's ideas, and those of other writers working in France, contrast with the work of many Anglo-American critics, and to suggest that they might very usefully be incorporated on a large scale into feminist criticism in English. The opening chapter specifically contrasts different readings of Woolf which use 'Anglo-American' and 'French' ideas.

Virginia Woolf is an important figure to feminist theorists and critics. Her book about women and writing, *A Room of One's Own*, published in 1929, is a popular and very influential text. Much of it is a historical survey of how women have lacked the opportunity to become writers, from the time of Shakespeare to the book's present time, the 1920s. It demonstrates that they have been prevented from writing by domestic and financial circumstance, and its title indicates that in order to write a woman must have private space, as well as her own income. But parts of it also conclude that some women have not written because they have lacked the appropriate literary models, and indeed a written language appropriate to themselves. 'We think back through our mothers if we are women', Woolf wrote, and 'it is useless to go to the great men writers for help, however much one may go to them for pleasure.'[48] This is a section of *A Room of One's Own* which carries great conviction for many feminist critics, who still face a world in which writers and other experts are more often men than women. It articulates in a clear image their idea of gender difference itself: their conviction that it is an aspect of how we all think, not simply an immutable physical difference. *A Room of One's Own* shows that there is no single truth articulated by great writers, but that 'different' people – women for example – seek to construct different truths.

During the 1970s and early 1980s, when feminist critics were first beginning to try to acknowledge women as people who write and think, *A Room of One's Own* was much more widely discussed than

Woolf's novels. Toril Moi deplores this. She argues that the theories of Lacan and Kristeva can be used to 'rescue Virginia Woolf for feminist politics',[49] and that Woolf's novels are as important for feminist thinking as her essays.

Moi's book polarises existing feminist criticism into two distinct groups, the Anglo-American and the French. She broadly character-ises Anglo-American feminist criticism as relying on the assumption that women write about women's experience in language that, whether adequately or not, is a representation of that objectively existing experience. Moi does not share this assumption. Early in her book she takes strong issue with Elaine Showalter whose *A Literature of Their Own*[50] offers a detailed account of a tradition of women's writing about women's experience. As Moi says, Showalter's chapter on Woolf is largely concerned only with *A Room of One's Own,* which is criticised harshly by Showalter because it does not confront or describe Woolf's own anger at her own life and her experience of womanhood. Moi accuses Showalter of a naïve insistence on the assumption that an author, thought of as a single and unchanging consciousness, should straightforwardly describe her experience in order that a reader, thought of as a passive receiver, can possess it too. Later Moi also criticises another prominent American feminist writer, Jane Marcus, for arguing that Woolf's work must be seen as feminist just because of what we know about Woolf's life.[51]

The French feminist criticism which Moi opposes to her account of Anglo-American work is presented largely in terms of the psycho-analytic theory of Julia Kristeva, Hélène Cixous and Luce Irigaray, who all, in different ways, draw on the work of Freud and of Jacques Lacan. Moi's discussion of Woolf in this context, in the essay re-printed here, explains ideas which derive specifically from Kristeva. The principal difference between the critical method Moi recom-mends here and the assumption she ascribes to Showalter is that the Kristevan view sees consciousness and personal identity as a continu-ing process, indeed a struggle, whereas Showalter is taken to see it as fixed. Woolf's writing, Moi suggests, shows the process, the struggle, of identity actually at work.[52]

This gives Woolf's fiction, as well as *A Room of One's Own*, a specifically feminist importance because the struggle of conscious-ness, the continuous process that is human identity, is bound up in psychoanalytic theory with the experience of gender. As Moi makes clear in her discussion of Kristeva's essay 'Women's Time', feminin-ity and masculinity are not seen as fixed biological states but as roles adopted within society. Kristeva defines three stages through which feminist thinking about gender might pass. The first is a stage in which women, assuming that equality of the sexes means similarity, demand equal access to power with men. The second is a stage in which they assert their difference from men and reject the dominant power system. The third is, or will be, a stage at which women reject the assumption that masculinity and femininity are opposites which an individual must finally choose between.[53] Virginia Woolf's writing, Moi claims, articulates ideals akin to Kristeva's third stage.[54]

But there is more to it than this. In another work of Kristeva's, 'Revolution in Poetic Language', to which Moi also refers, it is argued that certain disrupted kinds of writing associated particularly with modernism are 'revolutionary' in that they demonstrate resistance to an oppressive order.[55] This argument, as Moi applies it to Woolf, is in some respects similar to ideas put forward in Tambling's and Beer's essays when they indicate that Woolf's novels suggest both a grand and repressive social or philosophical order and a potential for its disruption. But Kristeva's theory, like Moi's account of it, relates specifically to ideas about masculinity and femininity. It relates the idea of masculinity to rational language and organising systems of thought, and femininity to that which these repress, to disruptive forms of consciousness. In doing so it draws directly on Lacan's psychoanalytic theory, arguing that humans take up a predominantly masculine or feminine identity because of their relationship to language, not because of biological characteristics. At birth the human child belongs to neither gender, it is argued, and has no sense of itself as a person. It is united with its mother, with whom it shares sensations. Gradually, however, language intrudes on this sharing and the child begins, in some sense, to *think about* itself. The more the child does this, and the better it functions in language, then the more it represses its early state and identifies itself in terms of power and of masculinity. But the more it resists language or is threatened by it, the more it associates itself with femininity. This theory makes femininity a wholly negative concept.[56] But Kristeva modifies it by suggesting that some people, and especially women, retain the maternal consciousness alongside language. Moi summarises this by writing that

> Kristeva also argues that many women will be able to let what she calls the 'spasmodic force' of the unconscious disrupt their language because of their strong links with the . . . mother-figure.[57]

Such a woman runs the risk of becoming mad if this disruption is too great, and Kristeva herself has named Virginia Woolf's suicide as an example of this.[58] Moi cites Septimus in *Mrs Dalloway* as a portrayal of a mind that does succumb to this kind of chaos.[59] But Moi also follows Kristeva by suggesting that disruptive writing, which she considers Woolf's to be, can be seen as a revolt against an oppressive patriarchal society.[60]

Many other feminist theorists working on both sides of the Atlantic in recent years have also, like Moi, welcomed and made use of Kristeva's work. Makiko Minow-Pinkney's book *Virginia Woolf and the Problem of the Subject*,[61] from which the seventh essay in this book is taken (p. 98 below), reads Woolf's major novels and essays in terms of Kristevan theory. She argues that they enable their readers to experience directly the dilemma of the feminine identity, which works both in language and in the maternal consciousness that language replaces. Minow-Pinkney's complex chapter on *To the Lighthouse* in her book[62] argues that that novel *appears* to offer an orderly meaning through symbols, like, for example, the lighthouse itself; but that it also tantalises the reader because its symbols are not really made to *mean* anything. The reader therefore both searches for a set of meanings in the novel, and feels that they do not exist.

Earlier in her book,[63] Minow-Pinkney rejects J. Hillis Miller's idea (see essay 3) of the coherent narrator in *Mrs Dalloway*, arguing that that novel refuses any one stable voice and instead offers various changing ones. Then, in the part of her discussion of *Mrs Dalloway* reprinted here as essay 7, she gives a detailed reading of Clarissa and Miss Kilman, and Septimus, as actings-out of the struggle between rational language and the inchoate union with the mother. This perhaps sounds forbiddingly theoretical. But the essay is an attempt to use, and explain, Kristevan ideas in parallel with a simpler kind of feminist criticism, one more like the 'Anglo-American criticism' objected to by Moi: a feminist criticism that looks for and tries to describe accounts of *women's* experience. Minow-Pinkney's discussion of *Mrs Dalloway* enables us to recognise in the novel a series of images representing emotional predicaments that some, at least, of us experience. For some women, including the editor of this volume, this very theoretical criticism also functions like the supposedly unsophisticated work of 'Anglo-American' criticism in search of representations of women's lives. It helps us to see the novel as a reflection of experiences that we had not previously been able to admit to, or even to define.

IV

Not all feminist writers who investigate psychoanalytic ideas rely, however, on Kristeva's. The eighth and ninth essays in this book, by Elizabeth Abel and Margaret Homans, are two contrasting readings of *To the Lighthouse*. They are both written by American feminist scholars and both explore other versions of psychoanalytic theory, not only for readers of this novel but also for feminist criticism itself. Various critics in the past, not necessarily feminist in any sense, have read *To the Lighthouse* in Freudian terms as the story of *James's* oedipal crisis. They discuss his love for his mother, his hatred for his intruding father, and his eventual reconciliation with his father as they reach the lighthouse together.[64] Elizabeth Abel sees that the novel also tells the parallel but contrasting oedipal story of Cam, the daughter who changes from identification with her mother to admiration for her father, but who cannot become like her father and is therefore doomed to a kind of silence. Such a reading differs significantly from Lacanian and Kristevan theory. Femininity does have a positive identity, in that Cam's story is the story of her struggle to articulate her female experience, her conscious memories of her mother, in language – even though the point is that she has ultimately to deny or abandon it.[65] Her memory of her mother is not a disruptive 'spasmodic force', but a defined experience. Moreover, Lily Briscoe represents, for Abel, a woman who *does* continue to articulate a feminine consciousness, opting to do this rather than to use the language of men.[66]

In arguing for this reading of *To the Lighthouse*, Professor Abel uses some ideas from object-relations theory, a form of psychoanalytic theory which has considerable currency among American critics. In a book she published after this essay, *Virginia Woolf and the Fictions of Psychoanalysis*, she suggests that Woolf, much of whose work she sees as an independent working-out of theories parallel to Freud's, herself developed ideas like those of the later object-relations theorists.[67] One of these, Nancy Chodorow, has specifically contrasted the significance for feminism of object-relations and Lacanian theory. Object-relations theory, Chodorow writes, argues that infants themselves develop their own sense of self *before acquiring language*; they form an identity by constructing an internal set of 'objects', or images of people and things, with which they develop unconscious relationships. Already gendered, the female infant gradually constructs a different relationship with its image of its mother than does a male infant.[68]

Margaret Homans openly rejects Lacan's and Kristeva's theories. Her book *Bearing the Word*,[69] from which her essay here is taken, argues that women writers have to cope with a threatening belief about representational art, including fiction, which they share with men. In Western thought, she writes, the idea of a writer's being able to represent life in art has usually included the idea of the absence of his mother. Her first chapter traces this idea, and the cultural adulation of maternal absence, through many major texts including *Genesis*, *Paradise Lost*, the *Oresteia*, Wordsworth's *The Prelude*, Shelley's *Alastor* and, at greatest length, Lacan's work. She then goes on to use the work of Nancy Chodorow[70] to propose a different way of thinking about the development of a writer's consciousness. Chodorow is taken to argue that a female child, already gendered, is more privileged than the male because she does not have to define herself as different from her mother. So Homans suggests that daughters should be thought of as retaining access to two positive kinds of consciousness: the rational and symbolic language that is necessary for participation in society, and the different language of the maternal union which is rejected by sons. She differentiates this idea specifically from Kristeva's, because she says the communication between mothers and daughters, though 'socially and culturally suppressed' as a result of social practices, nevertheless exists and can be retrieved. It is not inevitably and permanently *repressed* as coherent language develops.[71]

Homans's book opens and closes with discussions of *To the Lighthouse* which exemplify this argument. It begins with a brief discussion of the scene in *To the Lighthouse* in which Mrs Ramsay talks to Cam and to James after covering the sheep's skull in their bedroom with her shawl.[72] Homans contrasts the way in which Mrs Ramsay uses language to James, to *tell* him that the skull is still there though invisible, and the way in which she uses it to Cam. The language she uses to Cam does not carry information but is simply a communication of presence. Homans concludes that this scene demonstrates the idea that women can use a different kind of language in addition to the one which they share with men.[73] Then her book ends with the brief chapter reprinted here (essay 9). Her argument has similar concerns to those of Abel, for both investigate the idea of the woman artist, but Homans's conclusions about *To the Lighthouse* are different from Abel's. Homans sees Cam as Woolf's positive example of the non-representational language of mother and daughter, not as a daughter trying to use her father's language; and she sees

Lily Briscoe as denying the maternal language, as opting for representational art. Her point is that *To the Lighthouse* is ambivalent, even self-contradictory, about Woolf's own idea of women writers thinking through their mothers: it images Cam thinking in her maternal language, but it shows the adult artist Lily rejecting this language and it uses representational language itself. Readers of this volume should perhaps decide which of these interpretations of Cam and Lily seems more persuasive and, more widely, what Woolf's work can be understood to suggest about gender difference and language.

V

Psychoanalytic criticism has been a very prominent aspect of feminism in the late 1980s and early 1990s, and it has generated some stimulating interpretations of women writers' texts. But its complexity does alienate some readers. It is also thought by many to assume too easily that women automatically have important things in common, and to ignore the particular circumstances of particular women in specific times and places. Moreover, the dogmatic application of a psychoanalytic theory to Woolf's writing runs the risk of imposing a single closed meaning on it. As the essays in this book show, reading Woolf involves an awareness of the narration, and of the experience of reading itself. Any interpretation which claims to define what the novels *mean* must focus, instead, on ideas formed after the reading itself is finished.

Feminist criticism is not an orthodoxy, however. It is a process of experiment which tries to articulate some of what it is to be a woman, and it is nowhere near the end of its work. Rachel Bowlby's book *Virginia Woolf, Feminist Destinations*[74] itself employs a number of different feminist ideas, and it represents Woolf's own work as a series of experiments trying to define women's aims and aspirations. Bowlby's account of *Mrs Dalloway* in this book (essay 10) offers us a variety of images of women constructed in different discourses: in terms deriving from Freud, in a comparison between Woolf's work and that of Charlotte Brontë, and also in terms familiar to realistic fiction – descriptions of characters and actions in a particular time and place. Elizabeth and Clarissa and Miss Kilman are all seen as women with choices about the roles they will play in society, in the 'real' world – and Elizabeth's choices are wider than those available to her mother's generation. But these women are shown to be unlikely to make a single choice. They are, to an extent, oppressed or marginalised by institutions and ideas which are associated, as always in Woolf, with masculine power. At the same time they are able at least to fantasise about rebellion against the established society. Elizabeth imagines a set of careers for herself, and goes off with Miss Kilman partly in rebellion against her respectable mother; Miss Kilman is angry with Clarissa and also with her own identity; Clarissa relives her past and her relationships, before Dalloway, with Peter and Sally. Yet while they can continue to fantasise Elizabeth is also, at the same time, becoming a pretty woman; and Clarissa's party is a success and her role as society hostess is confirmed; and Miss Kilman's life will never actually change. There is, Bowlby suggests, a real difference made in the novel between the confident but single masculine identity, symbolised by Big Ben, and the fluid and changing feminine one, symbolised by descriptions of the more timorous sound of St Margaret's. The women do not fit neatly into any one role or image of themselves – any more, indeed, than Woolf's novels can be reduced to a single meaning.

The ten essays in this New Casebook show that *Mrs Dalloway* and *To the Lighthouse* are directly about important issues of the society of their day, and of ours. These novels examine the implications of the First World War, and of the British Empire. They explore ideas about what a human being is and what the relations are between individuals and the institutions of society. Most importantly, perhaps, they are about women: about the roles available to them, and the ways in which they might think about themselves. But the novels also raise questions, which earlier critics did not follow, about narrative fiction itself. Especially, they challenge the illusion that the events in a novel existed before it was written, are being described by a consistent voice, and can be judged confidently. As we read Woolf's work we find ourselves to be participants in unresolved debates about war, empire, domestic life, sexual identity, writing, and ideas of human and political consciousness; and, more than this, we have to recognise and live out the complex activity of narration, of relating and explaining events, that we frequently take entirely for granted. Woolf is an author who has been marginalised and even dismissed, but her work is now seen to be at the centre of twentieth-century writing.

NOTES

1. *Mrs Dalloway* was published in May 1925 and *To the Lighthouse* in May 1927, both by the Hogarth Press in London and by Harcourt Brace in New York. There are variations between the British and American editions.

2. Some early reviews and discussions of Woolf's work were reprinted in Robin Majumdar and Allen McLaurin (eds), *Virginia Woolf, the Critical Heritage* (London and Boston, 1975).

3. 'After *To the Lighthouse*', *Scrutiny*, 10: 3 (January 1942), 295–8.

4. '*Virginia Woolf*', The Rede Lecture delivered in the Senate House, Cambridge, 1941; reprinted in *Two Cheers for Democracy* (London, 1951; Harmondsworth, 1965), pp. 249–65.

5. James Naremore, *The World Without a Self. Virginia Woolf and the Novel* (New Haven and London, 1973), p. 2.

6. Erich Auerbach, *Mimesis. The Representation of Reality in Western Literature* (Berne, Switzerland, 1946; trans. William Trask, New York, 1953); Chapter 20, 'The Brown Stocking' (New York, 1957 edition), pp. 463–88.

7. Virginia Woolf, *To the Lighthouse*, Penguin edition with text edited by Stella McNichol and an Introduction and Notes by Hermoine Lee (London, 1992), pp. 31–5. All further references to *To the Lighthouse* in this Introduction relate to this edition.

8. Morris Beja (ed.), *Virginia Woolf, To the Lighthouse*, Casebook (London, 1970), pp. 105–32.

9. *To the Lighthouse*, pp. 33–4.

10. Auerbach, *Mimesis* (New York, 1957), pp. 469–70; Beja (ed.), *To the Lighthouse*, Casebook, pp. 112–13.

11. David Lodge, *The Modes of Modern Writing. Metaphor, Metonymy, and the Typology of Modern Literature* (London, 1977).

12. See pp. 36–8 below.

13. Lodge, *Modes of Modern Writing*, pp. 73–7.

14. Virginia Woolf, *The Voyage Out* (London, 1915).

15. Virginia Woolf, *The Waves* (London, 1931).

16. See pp. 27–8 below.

17. See p. 26 below.

18. See p. 27 below.

19. See pp. 34–5 below.

20. See p. 36 below.

21. *To the Lighthouse*, p. 7.

22. Ibid., p. 19.

23. Ibid., pp. 9–10.

24. Ibid., p. 11.

25. Ibid., p. 19.

26. Ibid., pp. 37–8.

27. Ibid., pp. 69–72; section 11 of 'The Window'.

28. Ibid., pp. 90–121; section 17 of 'The Window'.

29. Ibid., p. 134.

30. See p. 36 below.

31. See p. 38 below.

32. See pp. 39–44 below. The original essay has further sections, not reprinted here, in which the argument about the centrality of James's story is pursued: see Gabriel Josipovici (ed.), *The Modern English Novel: The Reader, The Writer and the Work* (London, 1976), pp. 162–85.

33. Bowlby defines this as 'the most visible subject of the novel', p. 147 below. Miller draws specific attention to it as 'the "story" of *Mrs Dalloway*' in a later part of his essay not reprinted here: see J. Hillis Miller, *Fiction and Repetition. Seven English Novels* (Cambridge, Mass., and Oxford, 1982), p. 188.

34. See p. 46 below.

35. See pp. 47–9 below.

36. The Prime Minister in June 1923 was Stanley Baldwin, but the novel avoids a definite identification. Lady Bruton, however, is made to suggest the imminence of a Labour government (*Mrs Dalloway*, Penguin edition 1992, p. 121), and indeed Ramsay MacDonald became the first Labour Prime Minister in January 1924.

    This, and all further references to *Mrs Dalloway* in this Introduction, relate to the Penguin edition, with text edited by Stella McNichol and an Introduction and Notes by Elaine Showalter (London, 1992).

37. An earlier critic who was usually concerned to relate novels to the social conditions of their time, Arnold Kettle, dismissed Woolf as a writer about things that were neither 'interesting nor important': see 'Virginia Woolf' in his *Introduction to the English Novel*, vol. 2, *Henry James to the Present Day* (London, 1953), pp. 91–9.

38. Lyndall Gordon makes this connection and discusses Woolf's rejection

of popular ways of writing about war in her biography, *Virginia Woolf, A Writer's Life* (Oxford and New York, 1986), pp. 161–5. Other discussions of the novel's reference to the war and the changes it brought about include John Burt, 'Irreconcilable Habits of Thought in *A Room of One's Own* and *To the Lighthouse*', *ELH* (*English Literary History*), 49 (1982), 889–907; and Marianne Dekoven, 'History as Suppressed Referent in Modernist Fiction', *ELH*, 51 (1984), 137–52; and Gillian Beer, 'The Island and the Aeroplane: The Case of Virginia Woolf' in Homi K. Bhabha (ed.), *Nation and Narration* (London and New York, 1990), pp. 265–90. The television film of the novel by Hugh Stoddart and Colin Gregg, for BBC TV Productions in association with Colin Gregg Films Ltd (1983), dramatised 'Time Passes' specifically as the First World War.

39. See pp. 60–1 below.

40. Sir Leslie Stephen, 1832–1904, was a historian of ideas and a biographer, and the editor of the *Dictionary of National Biography*.

41. *To the Lighthouse*, p. 28.

42. See p. 74 below.

43. See pp. 78–9 below.

44. *To the Lighthouse*, pp. 225–6, and see pp. 83–4 below.

45. See p. 84 below.

46. See p. 68 below.

47. Toril Moi, *Sexual/Textual Politics: Feminist Literary Theory* (London and New York, 1985).

48. Virginia Woolf, *A Room of One's Own* (London, 1919; Penguin edition 1992), p. 76.

49. Toril Moi, *Sexual/Textual Politics*, p. 9.

50. Elaine Showalter, *A Literature of Their Own. British Women Writers from Brontë to Lessing* (Princeton, NJ, 1977; revised edition Princeton and London, 1984).

51. See pp. 93–4 below.

52. See pp. 87–8 below.

53. See p. 90 below. Julia Kristeva, 'Women's Time' (Paris, 1979), reprinted in Toril Moi (ed.), *The Kristeva Reader* (Oxford, 1986), pp. 187–213.

54. See pp. 87–90 below.

55. Julia Kristeva, 'Revolution in Poetic Language' (Paris, 1974), selections reprinted in Toril Moi (ed.), *The Kristeva Reader* (Oxford, 1986), pp. 89–136.

56. For a detailed discussion of Lacan's significance in feminist theory, see Elizabeth Grosz, *Jacques Lacan. A Feminist Introduction* (London and New York, 1990).

57. See p. 89 below.

58. Toril Moi (ed.), *The Kristeva Reader* (Oxford, 1986), p. 157.

59. See p. 90 below.

60. See p. 89 below.

61. Makiko Minow-Pinkney, *Virginia Woolf and the Problem of the Subject. Feminine Writing in the Major Novels* (Brighton, 1987).

62. Ibid., pp. 84–116.

63. Ibid., pp. 56–9.

64. Examples are: Joseph L. Blotner, 'Mythic Patterns in *To the Lighthouse*' in Morris Beja (ed.), *Virginia Woolf, To the Lighthouse*, Casebook (London, 1970), pp. 169–88; Glenn Pederson, 'Vision in *To the Lighthouse*', *PMLA*, 73 (1958), 585–600; Maria DiBattista, *Virginia Woolf's Major Novels: The Fables of Anon* (New Haven, Conn. and London, 1980); and part IV of John Mepham, 'Figures of Desire, Narration and Fiction in *To the Lighthouse*', in Gabriel Josipovici (ed.), *The Modern English Novel. The Reader, the Writer and the Work* (London, 1976), pp. 162–9.

65. See p. 118 below.

66. See p. 127 below.

67. Elizabeth Abel, *Virginia Woolf and the Fictions of Psychoanalysis* (Chicago and London, 1989), p. 133, n. 9.

68. Nancy Chodorow, 'Feminism and Difference: Gender, Relation, and Difference in Psychoanalytic Perspective', in Mary Roth Walsh (ed.), *The Psychology of Women. Ongoing Debates* (New Haven and London, 1987), pp. 249–64.

69. Margaret Homans, *Bearing the Word. Language and Female Experience in Nineteenth-Century Women's Writing* (Chicago and London, 1986).

70. Especially, Nancy Chodorow, *The Reproduction of Mothering: Psychoanalysis and the Sociology of Gender* (Berkeley, Ca., 1978).

71. *Bearing the Word*, pp. 1–39.

72. *To the Lighthouse*, pp. 123–5.

73. *Bearing the Word*, pp. 16–20.

74. Rachel Bowlby, *Virginia Woolf, Feminist Destinations* (Oxford, 1988).

1

Virginia Woolf

DAVID LODGE

Virginia Woolf exemplifies very clearly a tendency among modernist writers to develop from a metonymic (realistic) to a metaphoric (symbolist) representation of experience. The essential line of her literary development may be traced through the following novels: *The Voyage Out* (1915), *Jacob's Room* (1922), *Mrs Dalloway* (1925), *To The Lighthouse* (1927) and *The Waves* (1931) (her other books being, most critics agree, diversions, digressions or regressions from this line). And surveying these five novels rapidly in the order in which they were written, flicking the pages, as it were, rapidly before our eyes so that the changes in narrative form are speeded up and 'animated' in the fashion of a child's cartoon book, it is obvious how the structure of the traditional novel, with its rounded characters, logically articulated plot, and solidly specified setting, melts away; how the climaxes of plot are progressively pushed to the margins of the discourse, mentioned in asides and parentheses; how the author's voice, narrating, explaining, guaranteeing, fades away as the discourse locates itself in the minds of characters with limited knowledge and understanding; how the unity and coherence of the narratives comes increasingly to inhere in the repetition of motifs and symbols, while the local texture of the writing becomes more and more densely embroidered with metaphor and simile. The distance in technique between *The Voyage Out* and *The Waves* is almost as great as that between *Dubliners and Finnegans Wake*. But although the two writers travelled, formally, in the same general direction, they were driven by very different sensibilities working on very different experience, and Virginia Woolf's metaphorical mode is correspondingly different from Joyce's. It might be said that whereas his writing aspired to the condition of myth, hers aspired to the condition of lyrical poetry.

Essentially her writing does not so much imitate experience as question it. It is no exaggeration to say that all her important books are concerned with the question that opens the third section of *To The Lighthouse*: 'What does it mean, then, what can it all mean?' (p. 159). 'It', of course, is life. And the question of the meaning of life is intimately tied up with the fact of death. For if life is, in itself, held to be good, it is always threatened by death and is therefore (if, like Virginia Woolf, you are an agnostic with no faith in an afterlife) tragic. On the other hand, if life is not held to be good, there is no point in living it and one might as well kill oneself. We hardly commit a critical indecorum by invoking biographical data at this point and remarking that Virginia Woolf's early life was darkened by a series of deaths in her immediate family, especially by the unexpected and premature deaths of her mother, her half-sister Stella and her brother Thoby; that immediately after her mother's death, and intermittently throughout her life, Virginia suffered acutely from depressive mental illness, and that eventually she committed suicide. A shrewd psychoanalyst might deduce as much from an examination of the novels listed above, for they are all explicitly concerned with the question of the 'meaning of life', and all involve the sudden, premature deaths of one or more of the major characters: Rachel Vinrace in *The Voyage Out*, Jacob in *Jacob's Room*, Septimus Smith in *Mrs Dalloway*, Mrs Ramsay and her children Andrew and Prue in *To The Lighthouse*, Percival and Rhoda in *The Waves*.

Either life is meaningless, or death makes it so: Virginia Woolf's fiction is the trace of her efforts to extricate herself from that existential double-bind, to affirm the value of life in the teeth of disappointment and death. Her answer, fragile enough, but delivered with eloquent intensity, was to invoke those privileged moments in personal, subjective experience when the world seems charged with goodness and joy – harmonious, unified and complete. Here is Mrs Ramsay at such a moment, presiding over her dinner table, and planning a match between Lily Briscoe and William Bankes:

> Foolishly, she had set them opposite each other. That could be remedied tomorrow. If it were fine, they should go for a picnic. Everything seemed possible. Everything seemed right. Just now (but this cannot last, she thought, dissociating herself from the moment while they

were all talking about boots) just now she had reached security; she
hovered like a hawk suspended; like a flag floated in an element of joy
which filled every nerve of her body fully and sweetly, not noisily,
solemnly rather, for it arose, she thought, looking at them all eating
there, from husband and children and friends; all of which rising in
this profound stillness (she was helping William Bankes to one very
small piece more and peered into the depths of the earthenware pot)
seemed now for no special reason to stay there like a smoke, like a
fume rising upwards, holding them safe together. Nothing need be
said, nothing could be said. There it was all around them. It partook,
she felt, carefully helping Mr Bankes to an especially tender piece, of
eternity; as she had already felt about something different once before
that afternoon; there is a coherence in things, a stability; something,
she meant, is immune from change, and shines out (she glanced at the
window with its ripple of reflected lights) in the face of the flowing,
the fleeting, the spectral, like a ruby; so that again tonight she had the
feeling she had had once today already, of peace, of rest. Of such
moments, she thought, the thing is made that remains for ever after.
This would remain.

(pp. 113–14)

The experience described here has something in common with Joyce's
'epiphanies' ('the sudden "revelation of the whatness of a thing", the
moment in which "the soul of the commonest object . . . seems to us
radiant"'),[1] with Yeats's images of 'unity of being' and with T. S.
Eliot's 'still points' redeemed from time in *Four Quartets*. But in
Virginia Woolf the moment is not, as in Joyce, a kind of sacramental
transubstantiation of the commonplace achieved by art: though sought
by artists in her fiction, the privileged moment is not exclusive to
them, and their attempts to fix it in words or paint are generally
unsuccessful. Nor is it, as in Yeats and Eliot, attached to a particular
metaphysic, guaranteed by Revelation, orthodox or heterodox. Lily
Briscoe undoubtedly speaks for the author when she reflects: 'The
great revelation had never come. The great revelation perhaps never
did come. Instead there were little daily miracles, illuminations,
matches struck unexpectedly in the dark' (pp. 175–6). The privileged
moment is, then, transitory and recognised as such by those that
experience it ('this cannot last, she thought'), and yet it transcends
time: 'It partook . . . of eternity . . . of such moments, she thought,
the thing is made that remains for ever after.'

Thus a kind of immortality is asserted and death apparently
defeated. But what kind of immortality? What is 'the thing that
remains for ever after'? When Mrs Ramsay dies, the memory of this

moment dies with her; for although she is as a person remembered with love and sympathy by her family and friends, they do not remember the particular moments that meant so much to her. In fact, at the very instant when Mrs Ramsay is looking fondly at Lily Briscoe and planning to marry her to William Bankes, Lily is consumed with a hopeless passion for Paul Rayley who has just engaged himself to Minta Doyle; and looking back on this meal many years later she remembers only the pain of Paul's rebuff, and the folly of Mrs Ramsay's matchmaking plans. The privileged moment Lily recalls in Part III in connection with Mrs Ramsay, 'which survived, after all these years, complete, so that she dipped into it to refashion her memory of her, and it stayed in the mind almost like a work of art', occurred on the beach with the usually unamiable Charles Tansley – 'Mrs Ramsay bringing them together; Mrs Ramsay saying, "Life, stand still here"; Mrs Ramsay making of the moment something permanent' (p. 176) – a 'little miracle' of which Mrs Ramsay herself was quite unconscious. In short, Virginia Woolf's modernist insistence on the relativity and subjectivity of experience undermines the redeeming power of the privileged moment, because the moment is never shared.

As an answer to the fundamental problems of life and death, then, the privileged moment does not stand up to very close logical scrutiny; but it is intimated, and celebrated, in a cunningly woven web of verbal nuances which deliberately keeps the reader's analytical intelligence at bay. The long quotation above shows the different ways in which the writing accomplishes this feat: the paratactic syntax, adding clause to clause in the loosest fashion, seems perpetually to postpone the moment when the sentence will commit itself to something final (note the preference for semi-colons over full-stops). The parenthetic references to banal events outside consciousness ('It partook, she felt, carefully helping Mr Bankes to a specially tender piece, of eternity') break into the stream of reflection, mitigate the tendency to metaphysical pretentiousness and make the point that the miraculous joy of the moment arises out of the commonplace, not from some transcendental source. And the figurative expressions are dealt out in such profusion, withdrawn and substituted with such rapidity ('like a hawk . . . like a flag . . . like a smoke . . . like a flame . . . like a ruby') that we take from the passage a hazy, synaesthetic impression rather than any precise image.

Virginia Woolf's mature novels – *Mrs Dalloway*, *To The Lighthouse* and *The Waves* – are all about sensitive people living from one privileged moment to the next, passing through intervening periods of dissatisfaction, depression and doubt. For this reason, they are essentially plotless. Their endings are false endings, or non-endings, which leave the characters exactly where they have always been, living inside their heads, doomed to oscillate between joy and despair until they die. Virginia Woolf closes each book on an affirmative up-beat – 'For there she was', 'I have had my vision', 'Against you I will fling myself, unvanquished and unyielding, O Death!' – but the cut-off point is essentially arbitrary, and it is clear that if the text were to continue another down-beat must inevitably follow. It is not fortui-tous that the presiding symbols of the two later novels – the light-house with its pulsing beam, and the waves breaking on the shore – have this same regular, oscillating rhythm, and are susceptible of bearing multiple and contradictory meanings. Arguably this oscillat-ing psychological rhythm makes Virginia Woolf's work ultimately unsatisfying because the affirmation of the value of life so often uttered is never really made to stick.

* * *

[In a passage not reprinted here, Lodge now argues that *The Waves* is both the most 'poetic' and 'metaphoric' of Woolf's novels and the most 'monotonous'; and he discusses the earlier novels *The Voyage Out* (1915) and *Jacob's Room* (1922) as stages in Woolf's develop-ment away from 'the formal constraints of the traditional novel' to the 'decisive step' towards this metaphoric writing which she took with *Mrs Dalloway*. Ed.]

Virginia Woolf had an interesting correspondence about aesthet-ics with the painter Jacques Raverat at the time when she was working on *Mrs Dalloway*. He suggested that writing, as an artistic medium, was limited by being 'essentially linear', unable therefore to render the complex multiplicity of a mental event, which he com-pared to a pebble cast into a pond, 'splashes in the outer air in every direction, and under the surface waves that follow one another into forgotten corners.'[2] Virginia Woolf replied that it was precisely her aim to go beyond 'the formal railway line of the sentence' and to disregard the 'falsity of the past (by which I mean Bennett, Galsworthy and so on) . . . people don't and never did think or feel in that way; but all over the place, in your way.'[3] As Quentin Bell remarks, 'it is possible to find in *Mrs Dalloway* an attempt of this nature.'[4] In our terms, the novel marks the transition in Virginia Woolf's writing from the metonymic to the metaphoric mode. Instead of lineality, simultaneity ('If *Jacob's Room* shows cinematic cutting and fading,

Mrs Dalloway borrows from montage and superimposed frames,' Carl Woodring has shrewdly commented[5]). Instead of different people in the same place at the same time (e.g. the hotel at Santa Marina) different people in different places at the same time (time marked by the chimes of Big Ben), perhaps looking at the same thing (the aeroplane in the sky). Instead of a life, or a voyage, a single day. Instead of authorial narration, the stream of consciousness in which events (i.e. thoughts) follow each other on the principle of similarity as much as contiguity – a June morning in Westminster, for instance, reminding Clarissa of mornings in her youth because a simile of children on a beach seems to her equally applicable to both:

> And then, thought Clarissa Dalloway, what a morning – fresh as if issued to children on a beach.
>   What a lark! What a plunge! For so it had always seemed to her when, with a little squeak of the hinges, which she could hear now, she had burst open the French windows and plunged at Bourton into the open air. How fresh, how calm, stiller than this of course, the air was in the early morning; like the flap of a wave; the kiss of a wave; . . .
>
> (p. 3)

[Here Lodge briefly compares *Mrs Dalloway*'s structure with that of the 'Wandering Rocks' episode of Joyce's *Ulysses*. Ed]

Virginia Woolf's abandonment of a linear narrative structure and her plunge into the stream of consciousness can be related readily enough to the avant-garde *Zeitgeist*. But it was also related to her personal concern with testing the meaning of life against the fact of death; for the privileged moment which she was to offer as a kind of answer to the problem could be only given proper emphasis in a novel of the new kind, in which the causal or chronological ordering of events was subordinated to rendering the impression they made on the individual consciousness, showing, in Lily Briscoe's words, 'how life, from being made up of separate little incidents which one lived one by one, became curled and whole like a wave which bore one up with it and threw one down with it, there, with a dash on the beach' (*To the Lighthouse*, p. 53). Going out to order flowers for her party, Mrs Dalloway feels that life is good. She loves 'life; London; this moment of June' (*Mrs Dalloway*, p. 4). Walking towards Bond Street she is troubled by the thought of death: 'did it matter that she must inevitably cease completely: all this must go on without her' (p. 9) but consoles herself with a vague myth of immortality: 'somehow in the streets of London, on the ebb and flow of things, here, there, she survived, Peter survived, lived in each other, she being part, she was positive, of the trees at home; . . . part of people she had never met; being laid out like a mist between the people she knew best . . .' (pp. 9–10). In fact, it is not so much the prospect of her own physical death that disturbs Clarissa as the death-in-life that overcomes her at moments of negativity, hatred and self-loathing, and that (we infer later) has tempted her to suicide. These moments are antithetical to the privileged moments of joy and love by which she lives, and both can be provoked by the most trivial stimuli. Coming back to her house from shopping, for instance, she feels blessed:

> It was her life, and, bending her head over the hall table, she bowed beneath the influence, felt blessed and purified, saying to herself, as she took the pad with the telephone message on it, how moments like this are buds on the tree of life . . .
>
> (p. 31)

But when the message proves to be one that injures her vanity and separates her from her husband (Lady Bruton has asked him to lunch without her) her love of life drains away and she feels herself 'suddenly shrivelled, aged, breastless' (p. 33). She goes up to her room ('There was an emptiness about the heart; an attic room') where she usually sleeps (or rather reads, late into the night) apart from her husband. This leads to a depressed meditation on her sexual frigidity which in turn yields to a reviving memory of privileged moments when, through intimacy with other women, she obtained an insight into erotic rapture:

> Only for a moment; but it was enough. It was a sudden revelation, a tinge like a blush which one tried to check and then, as it spread, one yielded to its expansion, and rushed to the farthest verge and there quivered and felt the world come closer, swollen with some astonishing significance, some pressure of rapture, which split its thin skin and gushed and poured with an extraordinary alleviation over the cracks and sores. Then for that moment, she had seen an illumination; a match burning in a crocus; an inner meaning almost expressed. But the close withdrew; the hard softened. It was over – the moment.
>
> (pp. 34–5)

The psychological rhythm of Peter Walsh is very similar, alternating between love and aggression, optimism and pessimism, life and death.

As a cloud crosses the sun, silence falls on London: and falls on the mind. Effort ceases, time flaps on the mast. There we stop; there we stand. Rigid, the skeleton of habit alone upholds the human frame. Where there is nothing, Peter Walsh said to himself; feeling hollowed out, utterly empty within. Clarissa refused me, he thought. He stood there thinking, Clarissa refused me.

Ah, said St Margaret's, like a hostess who comes into her drawing room on the very stroke of the hour and finds her guests there already. I am not late . . . – like Clarissa herself, thought Peter Walsh, coming downstairs on the stroke of the hour in white. It is Clarissa herself, he thought, with a deep emotion, and an extraordinary clear, yet puzzling recollection of her, as if this bell had come into the room years ago, where they sat at some moment of great intimacy, and had gone from one to the other and had left, like a bee with honey, laden with the moment. But what room? What moment? And why had he been so profoundly happy when the clock was striking? Then, as the sound of St Margaret's languished, he thought, she had been ill, and the sound expressed languor and suffering. It was her heart, he remembered; and the sudden loudness of the final stroke tolled for death that surprised in the midst of life, Clarissa falling where she stood, in her drawing room. No! No! he cried. She is not dead! I am not old, he cried, and marched up Whitehall, as if there rolled down to him, vigorous, unending, his future.

(pp. 53–5)

Septimus Smith, however, has decided that life is not worth living. Traumatised by the horrors of the Great War, he sees the world as an evil place from which he is anxious to escape, and he does so by committing suicide. Through the coincidence of his consultant Sir William Bradshaw's being a guest at Clarissa's party that evening (it is the only vestige of 'plot' in the novel), this stranger's death comes to her attention:

A young man had killed himself. And they talked of it at her party – the Bradshaws talked of death. He had killed himself – but how? . . . He had thrown himself from a window . . . She had once flung a shilling into the Serpentine, never anything more. But he had flung it away. They went on living . . . They (all day she had been thinking of Bourton, of Peter, of Sally), they would grow old. A thing there was that mattered; a thing, wreathed about with chatter, defaced, obscured in her own life, let drop every day in corruption, lies, chatter. This he had preserved. Death was defiance. Death was an attempt to communicate, people feeling the impossibility of reaching the centre which, mystically, evaded them, closeness drew apart; rapture faded; one was alone. There was an embrace in death.

But this young man who had killed himself – had he plunged holding his treasure? 'If it were now to die, 'twere now to be most happy,' she had said to herself once, coming down, in white.

(pp. 201–2)

It will be noted that this passage echoes words and ideas in the two long quotations preceding: the moments of 'close' intimacy, of rapture, that Clarissa has fleetingly experienced with other women, and Peter's memory of Clarissa coming downstairs in a white dress. Peter had then a vision of Clarissa 'falling dead where she stood in her drawing room'. But it is Septimus who, in a sense, dies in her drawing room ('"A young man had killed himself." Oh! thought Clarissa, in the middle of my party, here's death' [p. 201]). And Clarissa feels that Septimus has in a sense *died in her place*. For she has felt the same terror of life ('She had felt it only this morning . . . the terror; the overwhelming incapacity, one's parents giving it into one's hands, this life, to be lived to the end . . . there was in the depths of her heart an awful fear . . . ') but she has been sufficiently protected, especially by her husband, from seeking the final remedy. 'She had escaped. But that young man had killed himself.' Paradoxically she feels her survival as 'Somehow . . . her disaster – her disgrace. It was her punishment to see sink here a man, there a woman, in this profound darkness, and she forced to stand here in her evening dress. She had schemed, she had pilfered. She was never wholly admirable' (p. 203). Thus Clarissa accepts her own failure, and acquires a new tranquillity and peace. 'Odd, incredible, she had never been so happy. Nothing could be slow enough, nothing last too long' (p. 203). Yet at the same time 'she felt somehow very like him – the young man who had killed himself. She felt glad that he had done it, thrown it away while they went on living' (p. 204). This is the real climax of the novel: a moment of perceived similarity and spiritual substitution. And, as we know, it had an exact analogue in the genesis of the novel, for in Virginia Woolf's original design there was no Septimus character, and Clarissa was 'to kill herself, or perhaps merely to die at the end of the party'.[6]

From David Lodge, *The Modes of Modern Writing. Metaphor, Metonymy, and the Typology of Modern Literature* (London, 1977), pp. 177–88.

NOTES

[This essay is from the third part of David Lodge's *The Modes of Modern Writing*, which is a group of essays discussing the work of particular authors and groups of authors. Earlier in his book, Lodge, following the Russian linguist Roman Jakobson (1896–1982), argues that the idea of metonymy and metaphor as opposite poles of language can be used to theorise the difference between realist writing and modernist or 'symbolic' writing. Metonymy is described as involving the linguistic process whereby signs – words for example – are combined with other signs with which they are in some way linked or contiguous. It is said by Lodge to be predominant in realist writing, and also in film as opposed to drama, and in any cultural activity in which the mind is mainly concerned to *combine*: to combine, for example, the words of a text or the pictures on a screen with other known images of the 'real' world. Metaphor, in contrast, is described as involving the process whereby words, for example, are *substituted* for different words with which they have a specific similarity; and it is extended in this essay so that Septimus's death is read by Lodge (as it has been by many other critics!) as a substitution in the novel for Clarissa's: Septimus becomes a metaphor for, a substitute for, Clarissa. Readers should judge for themselves how convincing they find Lodge's argument here that Woolf's work becomes progressively more metaphoric. They should also compare Mepham's use of the opposition of metonymy to metaphor in his essay (pp. 36–8 below).

As throughout this volume, references to *Mrs Dalloway* are to the Penguin edition with an Introduction and Notes by Elaine Showalter and text edited by Stella McNichol (London, 1992); and references to *To the Lighthouse* are to the Penguin edition with Introduction and Notes by Hermione Lee and text edited by Stella McNichol (London, 1992). Ed.]

1. Richard Ellmann, *James Joyce* (London and New York, 1959), p. 87.

2. Quentin Bell, *Virginia Woolf, A Biography*, vol. 2, *Mrs Woolf 1912–1941* (London 1972), p. 106.

3. Ibid., p. 107.

4. Ibid.

5. Carl Woodring, *Virginia Woolf* (New York, 1966), p. 19.

6. Virginia Woolf's Introduction to the Modern Library edition of *Mrs Dalloway* (New York, 1928), p. 29.

[Daniel Ferrer has recently argued that this claim about the 'original design', which is cited by many critics, is itself a fiction. He suggests that it directs readers' attention away from the extent to which the doubling of Septimus and Clarissa, which is a representation of Woolf's own life, is enacted *throughout* the novel. See Daniel Ferrer, *Virginia Woolf and the Madness of Language*, translated by Geoffrey Bennington and Rachel Bowlby (London and New York, 1990), pp. 8–39. Ed.]

2

Figures of Desire: Narration and Fiction in 'To the Lighthouse'

JOHN MEPHAM

I

The traditional novel is a form of representation which involves the creation of an imaginary but well-ordered fictional space. Within this space are represented the relationships, the dramas and the destinies of individual lives. There is thus concretised within the fiction the play of forces and values in terms of which, it is assumed, the apparently confused and chaotic accidents and demands of human life can be rendered intelligible. The orderliness of the fabricated story, of the human adventures which take place within the fictional space, consists for example in the consequentiality of fictional objective and subjective events and processes (i.e. that one thing leads significantly to another); and in their conclusiveness (that they come to a meaningful end).

But the orderliness of the fiction involves not only this internal orderliness but also an orderliness of its telling. For a story to be told there must be, implicitly or explicitly, a teller of it, a narrator, or a narrative voice, the voice of one who knows. The narrator who tells the story does so in order to speak his knowledge. The story is thus teleological both formally and substantially. The fiction has an end in terms of which its beginning and middle make sense. And the telling of the story has a purpose, a purpose which is prior to and independent of the fiction itself.

But what if we lack this sense of epistemological security? What if our experience seems fragmented, partial, incomplete, disordered? Then writing might be a way not of representing but of creating order. This would be a specifically literary order and would not be parasitic upon any belief in an order existing prior to it. For example think about the memory one might have of a person one has loved. It is possible, quite independently of literature, to give shape to, to fill out, this memory. It might be assimilated into some religious vision of life. Or it might be brought into relation with one's commitments to some very elaborated system of values, concepts and symbols (concepts and symbols which provide one with a means of expression, which enable one to say what it is to be a man or a woman, a mother, a political leader, a priest). But without such frameworks, without such means of thought and expression, we might have the feeling that the remembered person escapes us, is ungraspable, cannot be contained in our minds except as a disordered flow of particular fragments of memory – we might have a sharp but all the more poignant memory of some particular scenes, some images, gestures, a tone of voice, haunting phrases, perhaps particularly significant colours and sounds. These memories might be experienced as suggesting some unity which we cannot grasp, as raw materials which we might work on, condense, assemble into a form of speech worthy of their object. Then we would feel, as it were, that there is something that needs to be said but that we lack the means of saying it. If writing could be the means of completing the half-finished phrase, or bringing together and thereby enriching the fragments, then writing would not be primarily the telling of a story but the search for a voice. Narration would not be the embodiment of some pre-existing knowledge, but the satisfaction of the desire to speak with appropriate intensity about things of which our knowledge is most uncertain.

In this essay I shall examine Virginia Woolf's *To the Lighthouse* in the light of these considerations. I shall focus on the relationship between the story that is told and the telling of it, between fiction and narration. Locating and identifying the function of the narration will help to clarify the notion of 'finding a voice', of relieving the pressure of things needing to be said.

II

How are we to distinguish between fiction and narration? The fiction is the totality of all implicitly and explicitly narrated events and processes taking place within the imaginary spatio-temporal continuum of the novel. The narration may not actually give an explanation of the fictional events but it will implicitly refer us to the kinds of causes operating in the fictional space as explanations of fictional events. When it is narrated that Mrs Ramsay died suddenly one summer we do not need to be given a medical report by the narration to know that it is implicitly attributing her death to (fictional) natural causes.

That there is an order of the narration which is different from that of the fiction is clear, even though it may not be immediately clear just what this order is or how it is functioning. '"Yes, of course, if it's fine tomorrow," said Mrs Ramsay. "But you'll have to be up with the lark" she added' (p. 7). This event opens *To the Lighthouse*. It is the first in the order of the narration. But it is not the first in the fiction – there are narrated later (in narrative time) events which precede this one (in fictional time). The narration of a novel differs both in content and in sequence, rhythm and manner of organisation from the fiction. The narration of *To the Lighthouse* includes the words 'said Mrs Ramsay', whereas the fiction does not.

Moreover the narration can bring fictional things and events into relations which they do not have in the fiction. For example it can figuratively relate them to one another. Of course figurative relations can also exist in the fiction, in the fictional subjective order, in which case the narration attributes this figurative connecting together of things to a fictional subject. But there does not need to be, and there usually is not, a complete coincidence between the figurative relations established by the narration and those established within the fiction. The order of narration is an independent order. Just what relation exists between the order of the narration and the orders of the fiction depends on the purposes of the narration.

The *telos* of the narration is expressed by the specific constructions of the narrative order. It may be, and this has usually been the case in the traditional novel, that the *telos* of the narration was to represent a *telos* in the fiction, and in this sense the order of the narration was determined by the orders of the fiction. But this does not have to be so. When this is so one could say that it is the general structures of objective or subjective reality as they are represented in the fiction which are dominant. It is there that meaning is located and will unfold, reveal itself. Real time, the time of human life, is taken to be teleological. 'Time may give you the right key to all.'[1] Narrative time, the temporal structure of the telling of the story, is determined by this presumed teleology of represented time. The story is the appropriate form for the presentation of the emergence of meaning in a human life if a life itself has the form of a story. 'I thought I should die. The tale of my life seemed told. Every night, just at midnight, I used to wake from awful dreams – and the book lay open before me at the last page, where was written "Finis".'[2] But if life is not like a story then the novel should not be so either.

The main explicit play of the narration in Part I of *To the Lighthouse* is between the fictional subjective order ('streams of consciousness') and the fictional objective or interpersonal order. The conversation with which the narration opens seems to take very little (fictional) objective time, but the narration of the first half-dozen of its spoken utterances takes place over twenty-five pages of text. The actual conversation is narrated in direct speech, and these few short sentences punctuate or interfere with the longer, more leisurely and expansive passages of subjective reflection. It is as if these spoken sentences were markers along the objective time axis, a background rhythm which marks the slow but steady progress of the fiction through time, an arrow pointing in the direction of the basic tendency of the narrative movement. Textually these markers take the form of the appearance of particular graphic devices (quotation marks) and syntactical forms ('. . . ,' said Mrs Ramsay) which contrast with the narration of inner thoughts and feelings. There are, as it were, two sequences of pulses, the one multiform (the great variety of verbs of attribution and other syntactic devices used in the narration of 'indirect speech'), expansive, irregular (some short but many long contorted sentences), a kind of surging movement of different durations and degrees of intensity; the other more ponderous and uniform (syntactically, graphically and phonetically), the pulse of the passage of interpersonal time making itself heard, a rather dour but regular and dependable kind of sound.

The narration has transitions not only between these two orders but also, within the order of subjectivity, between the point of view of one subject and that of another. These transitions in point of view are always, as it were, internally (in the fiction) motivated. One point of view gives way to another as a result of subjective or objective movements in the fiction itself. That is to say the transitions are managed by the narration 'metonymically'. There are two main variants of this transition mechanism. In the first case one flow of subjective thought arrives, via its own internal momentum, at some other person as an object of thought or reflection. This other person can then change from being the object to being the subject of the narrated thoughts. In the second there is a physical movement in the space of the fiction which brings someone into the field of perception of the carrier of the narrated discourse, and the narration, as it were, takes the opportunity to pass the burden from the one to the other as if there had to be some excuse for doing this, as if the narration were afraid to appear in its own right, to show itself powerful enough to make up its own mind who should speak and who remain silent. There is thus achieved a kind of smooth passage from one subject to another, from one point of view to another, the narration never lifting itself out of the fictional space, being always generated from within it.

For example Mrs Ramsay is sitting at the window. She is thinking about the meaning of her life, about her son and her husband. She hears her husband, who is outside on the terrace, burst out with a dramatic recitation of some poetry. Hoping that no one has heard him she turns to see who is in the vicinity, and seeing Lily on the lawn remembers that she had promised to sit still so that her portrait might be painted. The line of her thought has thrown up and related, kept in subjective proximity, her husband and Lily Briscoe. The narrative plays with this conjoined pair (they are physically contiguous now as well as subjectively), holds them together with Mrs Ramsay in one narrative sentence that seems to be in flight across the gap between them and has not yet decided where to land, and then settles on Lily, adopts her point of view and begins to establish a new train of thought. Not only is the narrative passed across space from subject to subject; it is also about to go off on something of a tangent, away from both the space and the themes of the conversation which has been its basic home until this point. This it will achieve by having Lily actually walk away from the scene. She goes down to the beach, carrying the narration with her. This is therefore something of a major transition; it is marked by the narration starting a new section. This is how this shift is achieved:

> . . . but she [Lily Briscoe] was an independent little creature, Mrs Ramsay liked her for it, and so remembering *her* promise, she bent *her* head.

> 4

> Indeed, *he* almost knocked *her* easel over, coming down upon her with his hands waving, shouting out 'Boldly we rode and well', but mercifully, he turned sharp, and rode off, to die gloriously *she supposed* upon the heights of Balaclava.

(pp. 21–2)

Mrs Ramsay's thought has passed on from her husband to Lily Briscoe. So when he appears in the first sentence of the new section as the grammatical subject ('he'), it is as if he hovers in the narrative, an object waiting to be picked up in somebody's attention; or a pronoun waiting to be bracketed, to be brought within the scope of some attributive verb. The word 'her' announces the impending arrival of the fictional subject whose turn it is to do the work. The syntactic continuity between one section and the next ('her head' – 'her easel') prepares and metonymically motivates a transition, a transition which is at last accomplished as the 'she' of Mrs Ramsay's attention becomes the subject of the thought about Mr Ramsay ('she supposed'). The new section can now settle down to its new sequence and its new point of view.

It is worth noting a particular feature of the management of narrative sequence in Part I of *To the Lighthouse* as contrasted with that of Part III. In Part I we find two short sections (sections 2 and 15) which have the function of re-establishing continuity after a narrative diversion in space and time. And we find one whole section (section 14) bracketed with round brackets and narrating a flashback. The episodes in the flashback are objectively and subjectively related to episodes narrated in surrounding sections. The round brackets fold these distant but related events back into the causal order in which they belong and emphasise, as it were, that any discontinuity has been in the narration and not in the fiction. In Part III matters are quite different. Here there are short sections in *square* brackets which narrate events simultaneous in time but in no way causally or subjectively related to the events narrated in the surrounding sections. With these short sections the narration contrives to establish a *metaphoric* relationship between events which are not objectively related. So whereas in Part I we find metonymic transitions and the narration of non-simultaneous but causally related events in round brackets, in Part III we find metaphoric relations established by the narration of simultaneous but non-related events between square brackets. Instead of the flashback in fictional time we find a kind of flashpoint of figurative intensity in which narration of one event comes to assimilate, to hold within itself, that of a distant event in figurative, and no longer causal, unity.

So, to sum up, we have seen how the flow of the narrative in Part I of *To the Lighthouse* from one point of view to another and from one point in fictional time to another is carefully motivated by the narration by its arrangement of continuities of thought between subjects, and by its arrangement of constellations of movement of the fictional characters in and out of one another's fields of attention. The transitions are solicited from within the fiction itself by the interpenetration of fictional objective and subjective orders. The narrative order never clearly and explicitly emerges in its own right, even though it is in fact very much at work. It covers its tracks by projecting into the fictional space the causes of its passage from episode to episode. It seems to achieve thereby a multiplicity of internal, intra-fictional perspectives which gradually fill out and enrich the portraits of the Ramsay family. But in fact this filling out would remain very partial, incomplete and disorganised were it not for the fact that the narration is, in a disguised way, also having its say, continually adding its own ordering and enriching powers to the play of forces at work in the text.

III

Who speaks in *To the Lighthouse*? The dominant narrative technique is that of indirect speech, or more accurately, of indirect bracketing or attribution. The content of narrated sentences is attributed indirectly to fictional subjects, it is narrated as meant by them. In the language of phenomenology it is their 'intentionality' which is the source of the meaning narrated. But the use of indirect attribution gives rise to an infiltration of meanings which do not have their source in the fictional subjects themselves. It is as if in the narration of fictional consciousness the narration has, so to speak, a double source; there is a contribution by the narration itself and a contribution by the fictional subject. Using direct speech there is a clear demarcation (quotation marks) between these two contributions; they can be clearly identified. A space always opens up for the narration to occupy with its commentary. It can have its say. For example if *To the Lighthouse* were more conventional and used direct speech with narrative commentary we might have found something like the following on the opening page: '"It is settled", thought James, "the expedition will take place", his boyish mind rushing impetuously into the future, his wishful imagination allowing no obstacle to form in reality to the satisfaction of his desires.' With indirect attribution, on the other hand, there is no such space automatically provided. We remain within the fiction and the contribution of the narration can be disguised, hidden away. Let us examine some of the ways this indeterminacy of attribution is operative in *To the Lighthouse*, always bearing in mind that the basic, underlying principle involved is that of the duality between the partial, fragmented, manifest subjective order and the semantic unity and density of the latent narrative order.

Consider the following example of 'indeterminacy of scope'.

> All the way down to the beach they had lagged behind together, though he bade them 'Walk up, walk up', without speaking. Their heads were bent down, their heads were pressed down by some remorseless gale. Speak to him they could not. They must come; they must follow.
>
> (p. 177)

The suppleness of attributive technique is such that the narration can, as here, accomplish a transition from one subject to others (from Mr Ramsay who gives orders to his son and daughter, who feel obliged to obey) with no recourse to new explicitly attributive verbs, but via the continuity of reference to the pronouns ('them', 'their', 'they'). From being the objects ('them') they become the subjects ('they') via a transitional sentence ('Their heads were bent down . . .') which is not attributed to anybody in the fiction but which yet seems to begin to speak on their behalf. There is a suppressed attributive at work (*'They felt that* they could not speak to him') which could equally be taken to have this transitional sentence within its scope ('They felt that their heads were bent down . . .'). But since this attributive verb is both suppressed and ambiguous in scope there is also another possibility; that this transitional sentence might be attributed not to a fictional subject at all, but to a narrative voice, a narrative voice which is so close to the fiction, so intimately identified with fictional points of view, and which so seldom emerges in its own right explicitly to carry the burden of intentionality, that it is as if its existence were a closely guarded secret. The indeterminacy of attribution is exploited throughout the narration in the services of the narrative order. It allows the *telos* of the narration to be quietly at work, working on and through the consciousness of the fictional subjects, and through the flow from one to another of them, while appearing merely to be reporting what they think.

Indeterminacy or ambiguity in the scope of an attribution is very commonly used, as in the above example, as a means of inserting into the narrative a figurative description. One might see the description as conflating a contribution by the fictional subject (whose attention selects the object and determines the outlines and tone of the thought) and a contribution by the narration which performs a figurative elaboration of the thought. The narrative contribution not only adds force to the description but allows it to be articulated, in ways to be examined below, with descriptions elsewhere in the narration, to be placed within the general semantic space of the text.

> . . . this sound . . . which for the most part *beat a measured and soothing tattoo to her thoughts and seemed* consolingly to repeat over and over again as she sat with the children the words of some old cradle song, murmered by nature, 'I am guarding you – I am your support', but at other times suddenly and unexpectedly, especially when her mind raised itself slightly from the task actually in hand, had no such kindly meaning, but *like a ghostly roll of drums remorselessly beat the measure of life*, made *one think* of the destruction of the island and its engulfment in the sea . . .
>
> (p. 20)

This passage is extracted from one long sentence (which lasts for nearly a full page) of extraordinary craftsmanship. The sentence begins in typical 'stream of consciousness' manner, narrating what Mrs Ramsay could hear at a particular moment one afternoon. In the section extracted here it slips effortlessly into the iterative mood, no longer narrating a singular stream of consciousness but giving the narration of the moment depth by locating it in the context of the generality of the subject's experience and its contrasting moods. The narration fills out, provides extra dimensions of meaning and association on behalf of the subject and from her point of view, in this case by expanding the temporal scope of the experience, putting it in touch with its history. There has been a repetition of experience resulting in a pattern of traces with which, each time, the renewed experience can resonate.

The attributives within the subordinate iterative clauses are 'seemed' and 'think'. Each of them *explicitly* brackets the immediately following relatively prosaic expression (repetition of some cradle song, destruction of the island), Mrs Ramsay's own contribution to capturing the meaning for her of the sound of the waves. And each attributive *implicitly*, ambiguously brackets an immediately preceding, highly charged figurative account of the meaning of the sounds ('beat a measured and soothing tattoo to her thoughts', 'a ghostly roll of drums remorselessly beat the measure of life') in which the narration speaks for Mrs Ramsay, saying, as do the poems she hears later that day, 'quite easily and naturally what had been in her mind . . . while she said different things' (p. 120).

Sometimes it is a matter of indeterminacy of subject. In this case the attribution, while suggesting that the intention has an intra-fictional and not a narrative source, does not unambiguously identify this source.

> Mrs Ramsay, who had been sitting loosely, folding her son in her arm, braced herself, and, half turning, *seemed* to raise herself with an effort, and at once to pour erect into the air a rain of energy . . .
>
> (p. 42)

In this passage an attributive verb, 'seemed', floats free. To whom did Mrs Ramsay seem thus? The word 'seemed' locates the ensuing intention within the fictional space (in a way the alternative 'raised herself' would not; if there is some seeming going on there must be someone in the fiction to do it), but does not provide a subject for it. The nearest candidate for the role of subject here is James, who is the subject of the immediately preceding passage and who is physically appropriately located in fictional space. Is the absence of explicit attribution here, then, merely a stylistic variation that poses no problem, since the search for a fictional subject to be the bearer of this thought can readily find James to hand for the job? In fact, however, one would hesitate to believe of James that he was the sole author of such a complex figurative response to his mother's movement.

> . . . a rain of energy, a column of spray, *looking* at the same time animated and alive as if all her energies were being fused into force, burning and illuminating . . .
>
> (p. 42)

This is not just a matter of psychological realism but of recognising a general principle at work in the narration whereby the narration, as in the above examples, both speaks from the point of view of a fictional subject, occupies his place, and gives expression in its own words to what is for him too dense a feeling to be captured in words. The narration provides him with his own voice, makes available to him, for example, images which he would recognise as expressive of the force and content of his experience. And in fact, in this case, there is a repetition of these same images, only this time grammatically attributed explicitly to James. ' . . . James *felt* all her strength flaring up to be drunk and quenched by the beak of brass . . .' (p. 43). But this explicit grammatical attribution hides an indeterminacy of another kind. 'Felt' has two meanings. In 'James felt X' there is ambiguity as to whether X is the object of his consciousness ('James felt a stabbing pain in his back'), or the cause of the feeling ('James felt the gamma rays penetrating the epidermis in the lower dorsal region'). This duality of meaning is certainly being exploited in the quoted passage in order to leave open the implicit gap between consciousness and expression.

It is also worth noting briefly an example of indeterminacy of mode. In this case the narration attributes meanings to a subject while remaining indefinite about the mode of consciousness involved. It may even be suggested that it is not consciousness that is involved at all, but something deeper, less accessible.

> Mrs Ramsay felt . . . some disagreeable sensation. Not that . . . she knew precisely what it came from; nor did she let herself put into words her dissatisfaction when she realised . . . how it came from this: she did not like, even for a second, to feel finer than her husband.
>
> (pp. 44–5)

The narration accomplishes the seemingly impossible task of putting into Mrs Ramsay's words a thought that she herself did not put into words; of making precise connections and at the same time denying that the connections had been made. The contradiction is, of course, not a fault of narration but its skill in capturing the subjective contradiction involved in what Sartre would call 'Bad Faith'.

' . . . she had had experiences which need not happen to everyone (she did not name them to herself)' (p. 67). This involves an indeterminacy of mode in that we are told that although Mrs Ramsay did not name to herself her past experiences she nevertheless somehow had them in mind. The narration enters with her into a conspiracy of silence, while at the same time pointing in a certain direction (by virtue of what we have heard that 'people said' about her).

We have examined some of the features of the narration of *To the Lighthouse* in order to reveal the presence of a narrative order and its modes of operation. This narrative order is an order of meanings, meanings which cannot be attributed to fictional subjects. It imposes order and density. . . . Moreover the narrative order creates density of expression not only by providing a trans-individual framework of meanings, but also by virtue of the fact that this framework is constructed simultaneously at many different *levels* of meaning. That the narration adds density of *metaphor* we have already seen. But the elaborate framework of metaphor is consolidated by the simultaneous exploitation of other means of expression in a way that is characteristic of poetry. The narration is expressive at the levels of figurative, phonetic, metrical and rhythmic meaning. The intensity of the narration thus has its source in a double unification: the unification of the voices of the various individual fictional subjects, and the multiple over-determination of many levels of meaning.

From *The Modern English Novel: the Reader, the Writer and the Work*, ed. Gabriel Josipovici (London, 1976), pp. 149–61.

NOTES

[This is the first three sections of John Mepham's essay on *To the Lighthouse* originally published in Josipovici's *The Modern English Novel*. The whole essay is concerned to argue that there is actually a very firm narrative construction in the novel in spite of the apparent absence of a conventionally authoritative narrative voice. In arguing this the essay implicitly contradicts the idea, voiced by Lodge above (see pp. 26–7), that the novel lacks plot or clear action. Mepham's last four sections, not included here, demonstrate this argument with a detailed reading that makes the novel centre on the story of James's oedipal crisis. His first two sections, printed above (pp. 33–9), set out ways of thinking about the narrative structure of novels in general, and of *To the Lighthouse* in particular. They distinguish between the imagined events or 'fiction' and the narration, the way in which those events are presented; they introduce the idea of the *telos*, the final point of a narration towards which all its episodes are seen to lead; and they compare the narrative movement of the sections of *To the Lighthouse*, especially of 'The Window' and 'The Lighthouse', in terms of the contrast between metonymy and metaphor. His third section (pp. 39–44 above) examines the construction of the narrative voice, beginning with the question 'Who speaks in *To the Lighthouse*?'.

It should be noted that throughout this essay italics in passages quoted from *To the Lighthouse* are Mepham's, not Woolf's.

As throughout this volume, references to *To the Lighthouse* are to the Penguin edition with Introduction and Notes by Hermione Lee and text edited by Stella McNichol (London, 1992). Ed.]

1. Charlotte Brontë, *Shirley* (Harmondsworth, 1974), p. 501.
2. Ibid., p. 542.

3

'Mrs Dalloway': Repetition as Raising of the Dead

J. HILLIS MILLER

The shift from the late Victorian or early modern Thomas Hardy to a fully modernist writer like Virginia Woolf might be thought of as the transition to a new complexity and a new self-consciousness in the use of devices of repetition in narrative. Critics commonly em-phasise the newness of Virginia Woolf's art. They have discussed her use of the so-called stream-of-consciousness technique, her dissolu-tion of traditional limits of plot and character, her attention to minutiae of the mind and to apparently insignificant details of the external world, her pulverisation of experience into a multitude of fragmentary particles, each without apparent connection to the oth-ers, and her dissolution of the usual boundaries between mind and world.[1] Such characteristics connect her work to that of other twen-tieth-century writers who have exploded the conventional forms of fiction, from Conrad and Joyce to French 'new novelists' like Nathalie Sarraute. It might also be well to recognise, however, the strong connections of Woolf's work with the native traditions of English fiction. Far from constituting a break with these traditions, her novels are an extension of them. They explore further the implica-tions of those conventions which Austen, Eliot, Trollope and Thackeray exploited as the given conditions of their craft. Such conventions, it goes without saying, are elements of meaning. The most important themes of a given novel are likely to lie not in anything which is explicitly affirmed, but in significances generated by the way in which the story is told. Among the most important of those ways is Woolf's organising of her novels around various forms of recurrence. Storytelling, for Woolf, is the repetition of the past in memory, both in the memory of the characters and in the memory of the narrator. *Mrs Dalloway* (1925) is a brilliant exploration of the functioning of memory as a form of repetition.

The novel is especially fitted to investigate not so much the depths of individual minds as the nuances of relationship between mind and mind. If this is so, then a given novelist's assumptions about the way one mind can be related to others will be a generative principle lying behind the form his or her novels take. From this perspective the question of narrative voice can be seen as a special case of the problem of relations between minds. The narrator too is a mind projected by a way of speaking, a mind usually endowed with special access to other minds and with special powers for expressing what goes on there.

The manipulation of narrative voice in fiction is closely associated with that theme of human time or of human history which seems intrinsic to the form of the novel. In many novels the use of the past tense establishes the narrator as someone living after the events of the story have taken place, someone who knows all the past perfectly. The narrator tells the story in a present which moves forward toward the future by way of a recapitulation or repetition of the past. This retelling brings that past up to the present as a completed whole, or it moves toward such completion. This form of an incomplete circle, time moving toward a closure which will bring together past, present and future as a perfected whole, is the temporal form of many novels.

Interpersonal relations as a theme, the use of an omniscient narrator who is a collective mind rising from the copresence of many individual minds, indirect discourse as the means by which that narrator dwells within the minds of individual characters and registers what goes on there, temporality as a determining principle of theme and technique – these are, I have argued elsewhere,[2] among the most important elements of form in Victorian fiction, perhaps in fiction of any time, in one proportion or another. Just these elements are fundamental to Virginia Woolf's work too. It would be as true to say that she investigates implications of these traditional conventions of form as to say that she brings something new into fiction. This can be demonstrated especially well in *Mrs Dalloway*. The novel depends on the presence of a narrator who remembers all and who has a power of resurrecting the past in her narration. In *Mrs Dalloway* narration is repetition as the raising of the dead.

'Nothing exists outside us except a state of mind' (Mrs Dalloway, p. 62) – this seemingly casual and somewhat inscrutable statement is reported from the thoughts of the solitary traveller in Peter Walsh's dream as Peter sits snoring on a bench in Regent's Park. The sentence provides an initial clue to the mode of existence of the narrator of *Mrs Dalloway*. The narrator is that state of mind which exists outside the characters and of which they can never be directly aware. Though they are not aware of it, it is aware of them. This 'state of mind' surrounds them, encloses them, pervades them, knows them from within. It is present to them all at all the times and places of their lives. It gathers those times and places together in the moment. The narrator is that 'something central which permeate[s]', the 'something warm which [breaks] up surfaces' (p. 34), a power of union and penetration which Clarissa Dalloway lacks. Or, to vary the metaphor, the narrator possesses the irresistible and subtle energy of the bell of St Margaret's striking half-past eleven. Like that sound, the narrator 'glides into the recesses of the heart and buries itself'. It is 'something alive which wants to confide itself, to disperse itself, to be, with a tremor of delight, at rest' (p. 54). Expanding to enter into the inmost recesses of each heart, the narrator encloses all in a reconciling embrace.

Though the characters are not aware of this narrating presence, they are at every moment possessed and known, in a sense violated, by an invisible mind, a mind more powerful than their own. This mind registers with infinite delicacy their every thought and steals their every secret. The indirect discourse of this registration, in which the narrator reports in the past tense thoughts which once occurred in the present moments of the characters' minds, is the basic form of narration in *Mrs Dalloway*. This disquieting mode of ventriloquism may be found on any page of the novel. Its distinguishing mark is the conventional 'he thought' or 'she thought' which punctuates the narrative and reveals the presence of a strange one-way interpersonal relation. The extraordinary quality of this relation is hidden primarily because readers of fiction take it so much for granted. An example is the section of the novel describing Peter Walsh's walk from Clarissa's house toward Regent's Park: 'Clarissa refused me, he thought'; 'like Clarissa herself, thought Peter Walsh'; 'It is Clarissa herself, he thought'; 'Still the future of civilisation lies, he thought'; 'The future lies in the hands of young men like that, he thought' (pp. 54–5) – and so on, page after page. If the reader asks himself where he is placed as he reads any given page of *Mrs Dalloway*, the answer, most often, is that he is plunged within an individual mind which is being understood from inside by an ubiquitous, all-knowing mind. This mind speaks from some indeterminate later point in time, a point always 'after' anything the characters think or feel. The narrator's mind moves easily from one limited mind to another and knows them all at once. It speaks for them all. This form of language generates the local texture of *Mrs Dalloway*. Its sequential structure is made of the juxtaposition of longer or shorter blocks of narrative in which the narrator dwells first within Clarissa's mind, then within Septimus Smith's, then Rezia Smith's, then Peter's, then Rezia's again, and so on.

The characters of *Mrs Dalloway* are therefore in an odd way, though they do not know it, dependent on the narrator. The narrator has preserved their evanescent thoughts, sensations, mental images and interior speech. She rescues these from time past and presents them again in language to the reader. Narration itself is repetition in *Mrs Dalloway*. In another way, the narrator's mind is dependent on the characters' minds. It could not exist without them. *Mrs Dalloway* is almost entirely without passages of meditation or description which are exclusively in the narrator's private voice. The reader is rarely given the narrator's own thoughts or shown the way the world looks not through the eyes of a character, but through the narrator's private eyes. The sermon against 'Proportion' and her formidable sister 'Conversion' is one of the rare cases where the narrator speaks for her own view, or even for Woolf's own view, rather than by way of the mind of one of the characters. Even here, the narrator catches herself up and attributes some of her own judgement of Sir William Bradshaw to Rezia: 'This lady too [Conversion] (Rezia Warren Smith divined it) had her dwelling in Sir William's heart' (p. 110).

In *Mrs Dalloway* nothing exists for the narrator which does not first exist in the mind of one of the characters, whether it be a thought or a thing. This is implied by those passages in which an external object – the mysterious royal motorcar in Bond Street, Peter Walsh's knife, the child who runs full tilt into Rezia Smith's legs, most elaborately the skywriting aeroplane – is used as a means of transition from the mind of one character to the mind of another. Such transitions seem to suggest that the solid existing things of the external world unify the minds of separate persons because, though each person is trapped in his or her own mind and in his or her own private responses to external objects, nevertheless these disparate minds can all have responses, however different they may be, to the same event, for example to an aeroplane's skywriting. To this extent at least we all dwell in one world.

The deeper meaning of this motif in *Mrs Dalloway* may be less a recognition of our common dependence on a solidly existing external world than a revelation that things exist for the narrator only when they exist for the characters. The narrator sometimes moves without transition out of the mind of one character and into the mind of another, as in the fourth paragraph of the novel, in which the reader suddenly finds himself transported from Clarissa's mind into the mind of Scrope Purvis, a character who never appears again in the novel and who seems put in only to give the reader a view of Clarissa from the outside and perhaps to provide an initial demonstration of the fact that the narrator is by no means bound to a single mind. Though she is bound to no single mind, she is dependent for her existence on the minds of the characters. She can think, feel, see only as they thought, felt, and saw. Things exist for her, she exists for herself, only because the others once existed. Like the omniscient narrators of *Vanity Fair*, *Middlemarch*, or *The Last Chronicle of Barset*, the omniscient narrator of *Mrs Dalloway* is a general consciousness or social mind which rises into existence out of the collective mental experience of the individual human beings in the story. The cogito of the narrator of *Mrs Dalloway* is, 'They thought, therefore I am'.

One implication of this relation between the narrator's mind and the characters' minds is that, though for the most part the characters do not know it, the universal mind is part of their own minds, or rather their minds are part of it. If one descends deeply enough into any individual mind one reaches ultimately the general mind, that is, the mind of the narrator. On the surface the relation between narrator and individual goes only one way. As in the case of those windows which may be seen through in a single direction, the character is transparent to the narrator, but the narrator is opaque to the character. In the depths of each individual mind, this one-way relationship becomes reciprocal. In the end it is no longer a relationship, but a union, an identity. Deep down the general mind and the individual mind become one. Both are on the same side of the glass, and the glass vanishes.

If this is true for all individual minds in relation to the universal mind, then all individual minds are joined to one another far below the surface separateness, as in Matthew Arnold's image of coral islands which seem divided, but are unified in the depths.[3] The most important evidence for this in *Mrs Dalloway* is the fact that the same images of unity, of reconciliation, of communion well up spontaneously from the deep levels of the minds of all the major characters. One of the most pervasive of these images is that of a great enshadowing tree which is personified, a great mother who binds all living things together in the manifold embrace of her leaves and branches. This image would justify the use of the feminine pronoun for the narrator, who is the spokeswoman for this mothering presence. No man or woman is limited to himself or herself, but each is joined to others by means of this tree, diffused like a mist among all the people and places he or she has encountered. Each man or woman possesses a kind of immortality, in spite of the abrupt finality of death: 'did it not become consoling,' muses Clarissa to herself as she walks toward Bond Street, 'to believe that death ended absolutely? but that somehow in the streets of London, on the ebb and flow of things, here, there, she survived, Peter survived, lived in each other, she being part, she was positive, of the trees at home; of the house there, ugly, rambling all to bits and pieces as it was; part of people she had never met; being laid out like a mist between the people she knew best, who lifted her on their branches as she had seen the trees lift the mist, but it spread ever so far, her life, herself' (pp. 9–10).

'A marvellous discovery indeed –' thinks Septimus Smith as he watches the skywriting aeroplane, 'that the human voice in certain atmospheric conditions (for one must be scientific, above all scientific) can quicken trees into life! . . . But they beckoned; leaves were alive; trees were alive. And the leaves being connected by millions of fibres with his own body, there on the seat, fanned it up and down; when the branch stretched he, too, made that statement' (p. 24). 'But if he can conceive of her, then in some sort she exists', thinks the solitary traveller in Peter Walsh's dream, 'and advancing down the path with his eyes upon sky and branches he rapidly endows them with womanhood; sees with amazement how grave they become; how majestically, as the breeze stirs them, they dispense with a dark flutter of the leaves charity, comprehension, absolution . . . let me walk straight on to this great figure, who will, with a toss of her head, mount me on her streamers, and let me blow to nothingness with the rest' (pp. 62–3). Even Lady Bruton, as she falls ponderously asleep after her luncheon meeting, feels 'as if one's friends were attached to one's body, after lunching with them, by a thin thread' (p. 123).

This notion of a union of each mind in its depths with all the other minds and with a universal, impersonal mind for which the narrator speaks is confirmed by those notations in *A Writer's Diary* in which, while writing *Mrs Dalloway*, Woolf speaks of her 'great discovery', what she calls her 'tunnelling process', that method whereby, as she says, 'I dig out beautiful caves behind my characters: I think that gives exactly what I want; humanity, humour, depth. The idea is that the caves shall connect'.[4]

Deep below the surface, in some dark and remote cave of the spirit, each person's mind connects with all the other minds, in a vast cavern where all the tunnels end. Peter Walsh's version of the image of the maternal tree ends nevertheless on an ominous note. To reach the great figure is to be blown to nothingness with the rest. This happens because union with the general mind is incompatible with the distinctions, the limitations, the definite edges and outlines, one thing here, another thing there, of daylight consciousness. The realm of union is a region of dispersion, of darkness, of indistinction, sleep, and death. The fear or attraction of the annihilating fall into nothingness echoes through *Mrs Dalloway*. The novel seems to be based on an irreconcilable opposition between individuality and universality. By reason of his or her existence as a conscious human being, each man or woman is alienated from the whole of which he or she is actually, though unwittingly or at best half-consciously, a part. That half-consciousness gives each person a sense of incompletion. Each person yearns to be joined in one way or another to the whole from which he or she is separated by the conditions of existence as an individual.

One way to achieve this wholeness might be to build up toward some completeness in the daylight world, rather than to sink down into the dark world of death. 'What a lark! What a plunge!' (p. 3) – the beginning of the third paragraph of *Mrs Dalloway* contains in miniature the two contrary movements of the novel. If the fall into death is one pole of the novel, fulfilled in Septimus Smith's suicidal plunge, the other pole is the rising motion of 'building it up', of constructive action in the moment, fulfilled in Clarissa Dalloway's party. Turning away from the obscure depths within them, the characters, may, like Clarissa, embrace the moment with elation and attempt to gather everything together in a diamond point of brightness: 'For Heaven only knows why one loves it so, how one sees it so, making it up, building it round one, tumbling it, creating it every moment afresh'; 'what she loved was this, here, now, in front of her';

'Clarissa . . . plunged into the very heart of the moment, transfixed it, there – the moment of this June morning on which was the pressure of all the other mornings, . . . collecting the whole of her at one point' (pp. 4, 9, 40). In the same way, Peter Walsh after his sleep on a park bench feels, 'Life itself, every moment of it, every drop of it, here, this instant, now, in the sun, in Regent's Park, was enough' (p. 87). (This echoing from Clarissa to Peter, it is worth noting, is proof that Clarissa is right to think that they 'live in each other'.)

'The pressure of all the other mornings' – one way the characters in *Mrs Dalloway* achieve continuity and wholeness is through the ease with which images from their pasts rise within them to overwhelm them with a sense of immediate presence. If the characters of the novel live according to an abrupt, discontinuous, nervous rhythm, rising one moment to heights of ecstasy only to be dropped again in sudden terror or despondency, nevertheless their experience is marked by profound continuities.

The remarkably immediate access the characters have to their pasts is one such continuity. The present, for them, is the perpetual repetition of the past. In one sense the moment is all that is real. Life in the present instant is a narrow plank reaching over the abyss of death between the nothingness of past and future. Near the end of the novel Clarissa thinks of 'the terror; the overwhelming incapacity, one's parents giving it into one's hands, this life, to be lived to the end, to be walked with serenely: there was in the depths of her heart an awful fear' (pp. 202–3). In another sense, the weight of all the past moments presses just beneath the surface of the present, ready in an instant to flow into consciousness, overwhelming it with the immediate presence of the past. Nothing could be less like the intermittencies and difficulties of memory in Wordsworth or in Proust than the spontaneity and ease of memory in *Mrs Dalloway*. Repeatedly during the day of the novel's action the reader finds himself within the mind of a character who has been invaded and engulfed by a memory so vivid that it displaces the present of the novel and becomes the virtual present of the reader's experience. So fluid are the boundaries between past and present that the reader sometimes has great difficulty knowing whether he is encountering an image from the character's past or something part of the character's immediate experience.

An example of this occurs in the opening paragraphs of the novel. *Mrs Dalloway* begins in the middle of things with the report of something Clarissa says just before she leaves her home in Westminster to walk to the florist on Bond Street: 'Mrs Dalloway said she would buy the flowers herself' (p. 3). A few sentences later, after a description of Clarissa's recognition that it is a fine day and just following the first instance of the motif of terror combined with ecstasy ('What a lark! What a plunge!'), the reader is 'plunged' within the closeness of an experience which seems to be part of the present, for he is as yet ignorant of the place names in the novel or of their relation to the times of Clarissa's life. Actually, the experience is from Clarissa's adolescence: 'For so it had always seemed to her, when, with a little squeak of the hinges, which she could hear now, she had burst open the French windows and plunged at Bourton into the open air' (p. 3).

The word 'plunge', reiterated here, expresses a pregnant ambiguity. If a 'lark' and a 'plunge' seem at first almost the same thing, rising and falling versions of the same leap of ecstasy, and if Clarissa's plunge into the open air when she bursts open the windows at Bourton seems to confirm this identity, the reader may remember this opening page much later when Septimus leaps from a window to his death. Clarissa, hearing of his suicide at her party, confirms this connection by asking herself, 'But this young man who had killed himself – had he plunged holding his treasure?' (p. 202). If *Mrs Dalloway* is organised around the contrary penchants of rising and falling, these motions are not only opposites, but are also ambiguously similar. They change places bewilderingly, so that down and up, falling and rising, death and life, isolation and communication, are mirror images of one another rather than a confrontation of negative and positive orientations of the spirit. Clarissa's plunge at Bourton into the open air is an embrace of life in its richness, promise and immediacy, but it is when the reader encounters it already an image from the dead past. Moreover, it anticipates Septimus's plunge into death. It is followed in Clarissa's memory of it by her memory that when she stood at the open window she felt 'something awful was about to happen' (p. 3). The reader is not surprised to find that in this novel which is made up of a stream of subtle variations on a few themes, one of the things Clarissa sees from the window at Bourton is 'the rooks rising, falling' (p. 3).

The temporal placement of Clarissa's experiences at Bourton is equally ambiguous. The 'now' of the sentence describing Clarissa's plunge ('with a little squeak of the hinges, which she could hear now'), is the narrator's memory of Clarissa's memory of her childhood home brought back so vividly into Clarissa's mind that it becomes the present of her experience and of the reader's experience.

The sentence opens the door to a flood of memories which bring that faraway time back to her as a present with the complexity and fullness of immediate experience.

These memories are not simply present. The ambiguity of the temporal location of this past time derives from the narrator's use of the past tense conventional in fiction. This convention is one of the aspects of the novel which Woolf carries on unchanged from her eighteenth- and nineteenth-century predecessors. The first sentence of the novel ('Mrs Dalloway said she would buy the flowers herself'), establishes a temporal distance between the narrator's present and the present of the characters. Everything that the characters do or think is placed firmly in an indefinite past as something which has always already happened when the reader encounters it. These events are resurrected from the past by the language of the narration and placed before the present moment of the reader's experience as something bearing the ineradicable mark of their pastness. When the characters, within this general pastness of the narration, remember something from their own pasts, and when the narrator reports this in that indirect discourse which is another convention of *Mrs Dalloway*, she has no other way to place it in the past than some version of the past tense which she has already been using for the 'present' of the characters' experience: 'How fresh, how calm, stiller than this of course, the air was in the early morning' (p. 3). That 'was' is a past within a past, a double repetition.

The sentence before this one contains the 'had' of the past perfect which places it in a past behind that past which is the 'present' of the novel, the day of Clarissa's party. Still Clarissa can hear the squeak of the hinges 'now', and the reader is led to believe that she may be comparing an earlier time of opening the windows with a present repetition of that action. The following sentence is in the simple past ('the air was'), and yet it belongs not to the present of the narration, but to the past of Clarissa's girlhood. What has happened to justify this change is one of those subtle dislocations within the narration which are characteristic of indirect discourse as a mode of language. Indirect discourse is always a relationship between two distinguishable minds, but the nuances of this relationship may change, with corresponding changes in the way it is registered in words. 'For so it had always seemed to her' – here the little word 'had' establishes three identifiable times: the no-time or time-out-of-time-for-which-all-times-are-past of the narrator; the time of the single day of the novel's action; and the time of Clarissa's youth. The narrator distinguishes herself both temporally and, if one may say so, 'spatially', from Clarissa and reports Clarissa's thoughts from the outside in a tense which she would not herself use in the 'now' of her own experience. In the next sentence these distances between the narrator and Clarissa disappear. Though the text is still in indirect discourse in the sense that the narrator speaks for the character, the language used is much more nearly identical with what Clarissa might herself have said, and the tense is the one she would use: 'How fresh, how calm, stiller than this of course, the air was in the early morning.' The 'was' here is the sign of a relative identity between the narrator's mind and the character's mind. From the point of view the narrator momentarily adopts, Clarissa's youth is at the same distance from the narrator as it is from Clarissa, and the reader is left with no linguistic clue, except the 'stiller than this of course', permitting him to tell whether the 'was' refers to the present of the narration or to its past. The 'was' shimmers momentarily between the narrator's past and Clarissa's past. The subtly varying tense structure creates a pattern of double repetition in which three times keep moving to-gether and then apart. Narration in indirect discourse, for Woolf, is repetition as distancing and merging at once.

From J. Hillis Miller, *Fiction and Repetition. Seven English Novels* (Cambridge, Mass., and Oxford, 1982), pp. 176–87.

NOTES

[Professor Miller is a leading exponent in English of critical theory and critical methods deriving from the work of the French poststructuralist Jacques Derrida. He has written three essays on Woolf's fiction which, together, form part of his long-term project of re-examining the implications of the kind of writing that has conventionally been thought of as realistic narrative description – writing in which a narrative voice appears to describe things that have already happened. The first of these essays is the interesting account of the relationship between characters and narrative voice in *Mrs Dalloway* of which the first half is reprinted here. (An earlier version of this essay appeared in *The Shaken Realist. Essays in Modern Literature in Honor of Frederick J. Hoffman*, ed. Melvin J. Friedman and John B. Vickery [Baton Rouge, 1970], pp. 100–27.) The second, '*Between the Acts*, Repetition as Extrapolation', accompanies it in *Fiction and Repetition*, pp. 203–31). The third essay, 'Mr Carmichael and Lily Briscoe: The Rhythm of Creativity in *To the Lighthouse*', appeared soon afterwards in Robert Kiely with John

Hildebidle (eds), *Modernism Reconsidered* (Cambridge, Mass. and London, 1983), pp. 167–89.

The introductory chapter of *Fiction and Repetition*, in which there are also essays on works by Conrad, Emily Brontë, Thackeray and Hardy, sets out its particular project as an examination of ways in which meaning is *generated* in the novels discussed, and especially of how it is generated by repetition. Writing and reading are thus *not* thought of as activities in which sequences of words represent experiences that have already happened and that exist independently of author and reader, but as occasions when experience is created. *Mrs Dalloway* is seen, in the whole essay, as a complex balancing and repeating of the past in the present (which includes the present act of reading), and of that present in the characters' and narrator's past, and of the dead in the living, so that it becomes an enactment of the possibility that the dead live. *Between the Acts*, in the next essay, becomes a complex enactment of thinking forward from a known past, an organised history, into a projected future; and *To the Lighthouse*, in the third essay, becomes an exploration of different ways in which humans create meanings, culminating in 'Time Passes''s demonstration of how language itself creates the illusion of individual consciousness.

As throughout this volume, references to *Mrs Dalloway* are to the Penguin edition with an Introduction and Notes by Elaine Showalter and text edited by Stella McNichol (London, 1992). Ed.]

1. See, for one well-known example of this, 'The Brown Stocking', an essay on a passage in *To the Lighthouse*, in Erich Auerbach, *Mimesis*, trans. Willard R. Trask (Princeton, 1953), pp. 525–53. [1957 paperback edition, pp. 463–88. Ed.]

2. In *The Form of Victorian Fiction* (Notre Dame and London, 1968).

3. See 'Written in Butler's Sermons' and 'To Marguerite – Continued', in Kenneth Allott (ed.), *The Poems of Matthew Arnold* (London, 1965), pp. 51–2, 124–5.

4. Leonard Woolf (ed.), *A Writer's Diary. Being Extracts from the Diary of Virginia Woolf* (London, 1953), pp. 59–60.

4

Repression in
Mrs Dalloway's London

JEREMY TAMBLING

Mrs Dalloway is set in 1923, so its protagonist, who is in her fifty-second year (p. 34) is to be assumed as having been born around 1871 – eleven years before Virginia Woolf. Mrs Dalloway's affair with Sally Seton, which occurred when she was eighteen, is therefore to be thought of as taking place before 1889; two years after the criminalisation of male homosexual acts (but not lesbian ones), and three years before Keir Hardie became the first independent Socialist MP. With Sally Seton who read Morris, she meant to found a society to abolish private property (p. 36): Morris had founded the Socialist League in 1884. Sally Seton's other theme then was 'women's rights' (p. 80), that topic of the 1890s. Labour finally became the official opposition in 1922, under Ramsay MacDonald, taking 25 more seats than the Liberals, and the election of December 1923 enabled a minority Labour party to come to power in January 1924 (Lady Bruton seems to anticipate this, p. 121). The Empire is under threat in 1923; the novel refers to the 'news from India' (p. 121) and presumably when Peter Walsh wishes to find out what 'the conservative duffers' are doing in India (p. 176) he refers to the agitation for independence there. In contrast Aunt Helena Parry remembers India in the 1860s (pp. 195–6), and Burma in the seventies (before it was made a province of the British Indian Empire, in 1885). Peter Walsh, who has had the same penknife for thirty years (p. 47), was sent down from Oxford in 1893, presumably for his Socialism (the echoes of Shelley, whom Sally also reads, are probably deliberate), and his

57

then love of abstract principles and his reading of science and philosophy (p. 55) epitomise a radicalism that he has not been able to maintain: the future has passed from him. Indeed, he reflects with surprise that journalists can now write about such subjects as water closets which 'you couldn't have done ten years ago' (p. 78).

Ten years ago, of course, is 1913: the irony of the remark suggests how far this London society has managed to say 'the War [is] over' (p. 4), as though it could never be an issue again. Significantly, Peter Walsh thinks in terms of the changes between 1918 and 1923, not of those changes brought about through the war itself – one of the major themes of *Mrs Dalloway*. This novel is usually treated in terms of its use of 'stream of consciousness', or as a meditation on time and on building up the person every day afresh, but it nevertheless incarnates a critique of Empire and the war, taking the state as the embodiment of patriarchal power, and the upholder of what even Richard Dalloway calls 'our detestable social system' (p. 127). Dalloway's comment echoes Virginia Woolf's record of her intention: 'In this book I have almost too many ideas. I want to give life and death, sanity and insanity; I want to criticise the social system and to show it at work, in its most intense'.[1] The novel looks back on a lifetime's history and anatomises the situation produced by the part that obtains in 'London; this moment of June'. It is not a complete account, and its vision of London is itself nostalgic. It takes no note, for instance, of the beginnings of the Americanisation of the capital which was also a feature of the interwar years,[2] and its social range is limited. Its sense of London is not distinctly different from the nostalgia and the myth-making that late Victorian, Edwardian and Georgian architecture evokes.

Westminster, which Elizabeth Dalloway finds neither serious nor busy – the point is made in contrast to the professionalism obtaining in Chancery Lane and the Strand (pp. 149–50) – is at the centre of the novel. Its symbol is Big Ben, heard repeatedly throughout the course of the day's events, its chimes death-like ('leaden') and its presence, like that of the state, pervasive. Its evocation of negative feelings in the novel focuses the critique made of the state, viewed by Woolf as the very embodiment of patriarchy, both assertive and restricting. By a set of metonymies which deserve further inspection, it now stands in contemporary media representations for both Parliament and the nation: although Virginia Woolf did not live to know how the emotional power of its chimes heard on the wireless in the Second World War acted as a focus for the nation, the novel startlingly anticipates this deployment of the clock for ideological ends. Big Ben tolled for the funeral of Edward VII in 1910, and its chimes ringing out the old year were first heard on the wireless in December 1923: moments noteworthy for their provision of an apparent, though imaginary, national unity. In the decade of unemployment and class differences leading to the General Strike,[3] such a simulacrum of unity could only seem more needful. The broadcast chimes may even find their analogue in the pervasive sounds of Big Ben described in the novel. The potential of meaning goes deeper than the novelist can know, suggestive even down to the fit between air-waves and the fictional waves in which the leaden circles of Big Ben dissolve – a seeming synaesthesia which becomes literal in the age of the British Broadcasting Company. Time's expression is not so much the existentialist enemy in this novel, as a part of the language of state-power which is felt to be threatening and minatory, and which clothes itself in its architecture and statues.

Peter Walsh's walk after leaving Mrs Dalloway's house in Westminster (pp. 52–60) provides visible illustration of the power of recent history and the state. He turns into the significantly named Victoria Street, opened in 1851, and the site of the Army and Navy Stores. The name, which appears later, when Elizabeth and Miss Kilman visit it, is also suggestive: beginning in 1871 in order to furnish the military throughout the British Empire, it opened to the public as a department store in 1920, evoking the omnipresence of the Services within public life. Walsh passes St Margaret's (restored by Gilbert Scott, 1878) at half-past eleven, missing out Westminster Abbey, later visited by Miss Kilman, who watches people shuffle past the tomb of the Unknown Warrier (p. 146) – again, a then new feature of London public ideology: the soldier was buried in 1920. But he carries on up Whitehall, and 'glar[es] at the statue of the Duke of Cambridge' (p. 55), Commander in Chief of the British Armies from 1856 to 1895 (and therefore during the time when Walsh was sent down from Oxford). The references to the Duke of *Cambridge* and Walsh leaving *Oxford* are lightly juxtaposed in Woolf's text, as though implying the easy association of the army and the academy.

As Walsh meditates on his past, he is overtaken by marching boys of sixteen in uniform, too young to have fought in the war and destined (since there would be no more wars) to become grocers, to 'stand behind bowls of rice, cakes of soap on counters'. Their expression is statue-like, 'praising duty, gratitude, fidelity, love of England' (p. 55). Since they have come from Finsbury Pavement, they belong presumably to the Honourable Artillery Company, the regiment privileged to march through the City. They have come to lay a wreath at the Cenotaph, again new: Lutyens set it up in stone in 1920. The regiment passes on to the Strand; Walsh comes up to Trafalgar Square and faces statues of 'Nelson, Gordon, Havelock', 'Gordon whom as a boy he had worshipped; Gordon standing lonely with one leg raised and his arms crossed, – poor Gordon, he thought'. Gordon, who died in 1885 (his statue, now on the Victoria Embankment, was set up in 1888), the fighter of the Crimea, of the second Opium War in China, and the hero of Africa, epitomises those values that Walsh cannot free himself from – despite his 1890s socialism. His past in India, his playing with the penknife, that symbol of awkwardness within the desire to be aggressively male – these things give the sense of an irresistibly returning patriarchy. Walsh's childhood hero proves more potent in terms of character-formation than his Oxford rebellion. In the spirit acquired by association with such war heroes, he follows a young woman flirtatiously and has a 'fling' (p. 60).

**

[There follows here a long passage, which has had to be omitted, in which Tambling describes the Westminster of 1923 – which seems old to us but which was new then, with the Victoria Memorial still under construction. Tambling's point is that the London of the novel is the historical London, which was then forming into the embodiment of a society which worships imperialism: and that that imperialism involves both homophobia and the veneration of an ideal of 'Motherhood' which represses all emotion and presides over militarism. The passage concludes with a reference to Septimus's final moments in which, no longer stifling his feeling for Evans and his own femininity, he 'becomes a more complete character'. Ed.]

Character, in *Mrs Dalloway*, is not something merely inherent within a person: it is the result of an interrelationship between individuals and the space they inhabit. Clarissa's 'theory' of the 1890s, expounded to Peter Walsh from the top of the omnibus in the new Shaftesbury Avenue, built in 1886, is that 'she felt herself everywhere; not "here, here, here"; and she tapped the back of the seat; but everywhere. She waved her hand, going up Shaftesbury Avenue. She was all that. So that to know her, or any one, one must seek out the people who completed them, even the places' (p. 167). One such place is the formal, public, squared-off London of statues in rigid poses which helps to form those who live within its environment. Here is the Modernist sense of character not as something innate, but produced from without, from the lived practices (which must include the ideology) of a society, rather from a deep personal subjectivity.

On this basis, what character does this London produce? An answer might be that it has the capacity to intimidate and create a character that responds to it in terms of feelings of inadequacy – hence the novel carries in it a prevalent sense of neurosis or hypochondria. Its first page mentions Mrs Dalloway's recent illness which has affected her heart; the third refers to the Whitbreads coming up to London to see doctors. Septimus Smith began 'weakly' (p. 94) and after the war is in a state of collapse which licenses the prowling attentions of Dr Holmes (the name implies the doctor's role as the detective) and Sir William Bradshaw. Bradshaw, whose name recalls the railway timetable (the irony is comparable to that against Baedeker in *A Room With A View*) and suggests his rigidity, has been practising for thirty years – Septimus Smith's age – and he has, like Dalloway and Whitbread, a wife defined by weakness. Lady Bradshaw's will was sapped 'fifteen years ago': she is forced to 'minister to the craving which lit her husband's eye so oilily for power' (p. 110) and at dinner parties she suffers from a disagreeable 'pressure on the top of the head'. A pattern of male control and female illness is established amongst the upper classes in the novel. The pattern is only reversed by Septimus Smith, who must be looked after by Rezia, until he concludes his life by suicide. Further victims of illness include Lady Lexham, who does not attend the party because she has caught a cold at a Buckingham Palace garden party (p. 184), and Ellie Henderson, who is obsessed by people catching chills (pp. 184–5).

Bradshaw is at the heart of this medicalised society, identified by Woolf with serving the interests of the militaristic state. He uses the power of the law in his consignment of people to mental asylums (p. 106); his worship of Proportion – a no doubt classical goddess – 'made England prosper' (p. 109). At the same time Proportion's allegorical sister, Conversion, is imperialist, engaged 'in the heat and sands of India, the mud and swamp of Africa, the purlieus of London'. Rezia deduces that Conversion, which conceals itself under the names of 'love, duty, self-sacrifice', 'loves blood better than brick' (p. 110). The appearance of monumental London – dignified, proportioned, the celebration in stone and marble of the big words which Conversion and the marching sixteen-year-olds use – really signifies the desire for power that stops at nothing, certainly not the bloodshed of the war.

But what kind of criticism is Woolf able to mount of this will to power in *Mrs Dalloway*, and why does she fasten so much on matters of what would be called hysteria (in Septimus Smith) or neurasthenia (possibly Mrs Whitbread, probably in Clarissa Dalloway)? An answer in the spirit of Michel Foucault would stress the privileged nature of the doctor's discourse in nineteenth- and twentieth-century Western societies. The doctor's knowledge, which in Bradshaw's case 'secluded lunatics, forbade childbirth, penalised despair, made it impossible for the unfit to propagate their views' (p. 89), is power and a means of social control, since it contains the potential to define each and every non-medical person. David Armstrong's *The Political Anatomy of the Body*, amongst much else, suggestively details the rapid increase within medical discourse of terms for mental illness from the 1800s onwards and into the twentieth century. He sees this as part of a whole construction of people as being potentially mentally disturbed, through the intensified power of that discourse. Thus in 1922, Sir Humphrey Rolleston, President of the Royal College of Physicians, pronounced that 'probably the bulk of patients in ordinary practice present some disorder, however slight, of mind, conduct or feeling'.[4] Neurasthenia, an illness characterised by mental fatigue (hence the opposite of hysteria, which involved over-excitement), was first diagnosed in 1880. By the 1930s, according to Armstrong, the term was dumped as a clinically useless description. Like *The Waste Land* (1922) which ends with Hieronymo mad again and contains what F. R. Leavis in 1932 characterised as the 'neurasthenic' passage 'My nerves are bad tonight',[5] *Mrs Dalloway* makes mental instability a dominant theme. In the novel the necessity is for the self to 'compose' its fragmentary parts into 'one centre, one diamond' (p. 40). Biographical considerations are involved in both Eliot's and Virginia Woolf's cases – Bradshaw may owe much to Sir George Henry Savage, who sent Woolf to a private nursing home in 1910 and again in 1913 – but such considerations are only part of the texts' larger historical story, involving the increased medicalisation of society, the readiness to label people as mentally ill, and the absorbed attention given to nerves and mental instability.

Mrs Dalloway certainly evokes a prevalent sense of neurosis; according to Armstrong, in the early twentieth century the word was taken to contain a warning of possible madness. The psychopathology of everyday life is visible in Peter Walsh playing with his penknife, in Hugh Whitbread writing capital letters with rings round them in his typically pompous manner (p. 120), or in Lady Bruton's slightly obsessive idea of solving the problems of unemployment by sending people to Canada. Even Mrs Dalloway's slightly arch or fey interest in fresh air – 'fresh as if issued to children on a beach. What a lark! What a plunge' (p. 3) – can be related to this medical discourse: Armstrong says that delicate children were now to be looked after in environments stressing fresh air and open windows and, from 1907 onwards, in open air schools. The obsession with order, or Proportion, includes Mrs Dalloway's strong class and probably sexual dislike of Miss Kilman, and prevents Richard Dalloway telling his wife he loves her. A further craziness affects Sir Hugh Whitbread, whose fetishising of his twenty-year-old silver fountain pen suggests his comfort with things, not people. The novel involuntarily colludes with the dominant medical discourse in seeing people in the light of the clinic, assenting to the individualising gaze provided by twentieth-century medicine with its sense that health is something relative and social, an objective towards which the individual strives, the attainment, in fact, of complete 'proportion' (p. 108).

Armstrong's argument substantiates Modernist perceptions of character. The development of the dispensary within local communities, which is where he starts, stresses the idea of disease as being in the social body itself, in the environment – not in the individual, but in the spaces between people. It is less a question of quarantining and separation of people from a society – in that sense, Armstrong could be used to imply that Sir William Bradshaw belongs to an older system of thought in more ways than one – but rather one of seeing people as created from the outside. Mrs Dalloway thinks about the spaces between in relation to herself: 'Somehow, in the streets of London, on the ebb and flow of things, here, there, she survived, Peter survived, lived in each other, she being part, she was positive, of the trees at home [Bourton]; of the house there, ugly, rambling all to bits and pieces as it was, part of people she had never met; being laid out like a mist between the people she knew best . . . (pp. 9–10). She associates her existence with both London and her past home: she exists in the interstices between people and places and her character rises from contact with these things. The space between is what cannot be sealed off; there can be no hard edges of separation. General Gordon stands looking out as a lonely individual, but that isolation denies the creation of character from without.

Mrs Dalloway not only makes use of a discourse which reads people in the light of their secret and private diseases, but builds up a sense of their characters from that. As a novel, it cannot criticise that model of knowledge, however much it may despise Sir William. But the text implies that the prevalent neurosis may be accounted for in terms of a brutalising and destructive sexual politics. Armstrong is comparatively silent on the effects of the war in his discussion of the formation of a society known by its neuroses. Shell-shock and gassing could not be accommodated within the prevailing patterns of discourse. Further, the war issues from the social values seen in public architecture; and we have seen how the goddess Conversion not only gives doctors a licence to change people's lives, but empowers the state to destroy rather than to build up – to love blood better than brick. The feelings that the war harbours include the displaced homoeroticism of the Smith–Evans relationship. Paul Fussell's *The Great War and Modern Memory* aptly suggests the unrecognised homosexuality underpinning officer–men relationships: feelings that cannot be acknowledged, but which because they can be translated into myths of innocent and doomed soldier-boys do nothing to prevent the continuance of the war. Destruction is sustained through images of sacrifice and the unwillingness to allow innocence to change into experience. Boys coming into the trenches must not return from the battlefield into the dull working-class existences from which they had, superficially, been freed – which Peter Walsh envisages for the sixteen-year-old members of the regiment.[6] These homoerotic feelings are denied at a conscious level. That they are so is, in Woolf's terms, the result of the dealings of Proportion, which imposes identity, but which Mrs Dalloway left to herself knows to be labile: 'she would not say of any one in the world now that they were this or were that . . . she would not say of Peter, she would not say of herself, I am this, I am that' (pp. 8, 9).

To suggest that male and female homosexuality are at the heart of the book helps us to fill out the text's gaps and silences. The text, however, works by indirections as well as by unconscious motives, some of which Woolf is aware of, some not. The Miss Kilman/ Elizabeth relationship (the implications of Miss Kilman's name are polyvalent) and the Clarissa/Sally Seton memories both present cases of mutual female attraction which parallel the male feelings of Smith and Evans. In the 1928 Preface to the novel, Woolf wrote that 'in the first version, Septimus who later is intended to be her [Mrs Dalloway's] double, had no existence, and Mrs Dalloway was originally to kill herself at the end of the party'. The neurosis making suicide so potent a possibility in the text is less important than the fact that sexual difference – the male/female distinction – is, for Woolf, in no way fast and definite, but constructed. Septimus Smith emerges out of a potential in Mrs Dalloway. The novel questions how much the characters may recognise these differences as socially constructed, maintained through the patriarchal discourse of Sir William, for whom the distinction between normal and marginal behaviour is to be violently maintained by the imposition of willpower, and by the relegation or 'conversion' of the person who feels differently.

Yet Mrs Dalloway feels herself misnamed within her culture. She goes upstairs to her narrow bed, which itself anticipates a death-bed, and where she has been reading Baron Marbot's *Memoirs* the night before – memoirs being texts composed in order to guarantee that the person writing them is the same as the person who has experienced such things, making it possible to say, 'I am this, I am that':

> Lying there reading, for she slept badly, she could not dispel a virginity preserved through childbirth which clung to her like a sheet. Lovely in girlhood, suddenly there came a moment – for example on the river beneath the woods at Cliveden – when, through some contraction of this cold spirit, she had failed him. . . . She could see what she lacked. It was not beauty; it was not mind. It was something central which permeated; something warm which broke up surfaces and rippled the cold contact of man and woman, or of women together. For *that* she could dimly perceive. . . . she could not resist sometimes yielding to the charms of a woman . . . confessing, as to her they often did, some scrape, some folly. And . . . she did undoubtedly then feel what men felt. Only for a moment, but it was enough.
>
> (p. 34)

As with Madame Bovary, in Flaubert's novel, an irony attaches itself to the married name of Mrs Dalloway since it can never be uniquely descriptive. Further, the name 'Mrs Richard Dalloway' (p. 11) misnames. But the name 'Clarissa', a silent other possible title for the heroine (and the novel), suggests a mode of resistance to male aggression that Mrs Dalloway does not know, though it belongs to the novel's frame of references. It evokes both the social satire of *The Rape of the Lock* and Richardson's heroine, who dies after being violated. But although through some unconscious process Woolf harks back to two texts depicting rape in comic or tragic modes, Mrs Dalloway, despite having a daughter, still feels herself essentially virginal. The sensed alliance between this 'narrow' bed and her death-bed implies both a contrast and a similarity to Clarissa Harlowe, whose loss of virginity ties itself immediately to the prospect of death, just as her loss is the 'contact of man and woman' and (with Anna Howe) 'women together'. Mrs Dalloway is a marginalised figure in her attic: the echo of Bertha Mason in *Jane Eyre* is also perhaps present (it is worth recalling the use of that novel in *A Room of One's Own*). But if there is something deathlike about the state of women in this meditation, as the bed-linen is white, and Mrs Dalloway has grown very white since her illness (p. 4), she fits with other nineteenth-century women in white, fictional or real: Miss Havisham, Ann Catherick (*The Woman in White*), and Emily Dickinson who dressed in white, all victimised figures of virginity, of madness – hysterical or neurasthenic – and of confinement; indeed, all faintly relating to Clarissa Harlowe herself.

Mrs Dalloway herself is aware of a personal 'coldness'. The text does not require us to share in her self-blame, or agree that warmth is what Mrs Dalloway lacks in her relations with her husband. The criticism is self-deprecating, in a way fitting with a dominant medical discourse which defines sexuality and codifies what a woman's response should be to a man. The 'virginity' of Clarissa Dalloway indicates that the contacts between men and women are inherently 'cold' in this society, as are those between women. The point is glossed in *A Room of One's Own*: 'I am reminded by dipping into newspapers and novels and biographies that when a woman speaks to women she should have something very unpleasant up her sleeve. Women are hard on women. Women dislike women'.[7] It is not a matter of what qualities personally inhere in Clarissa Dalloway: rather, that a coldness, according to Woolf, exists in the codes of behaviour dictated by the way sexual difference is defined, between women. Sexual difference fits with class differences too: much of Mrs Dalloway's and Miss Kilman's mutual dislike is due to the class distinction making a warmth between the two women impossible. Mrs Dalloway has noticed the coldness in herself: the effect upon her is of a feeling of guilt, and of personal inadequacy.

The central, warming 'something' which could amend the coldness would have to 'break up surfaces', and this would involve refusing to accept not only the terms in which sexual difference presents itself – but also the dominant forms of London's formal late Victorian and Edwardian architecture, with its insistent ideological representations of power, duty and self-sacrifice. In describing this 'something', Woolf is glancing at her own writing: at the need for a text which would cut at those hard distinctions, beginning with the point that the 'androgynous' (the word is taken from Coleridge) mind is 'resonant and porous; that it transmits emotions without impediment; that it is naturally creative, incandescent and undivided'.[8] Thus any attempt to make difference stick is likely to be arbitrary and wilful. Androgyny, in its traditional sense of 'combining the attributes of both sexes', suggests an essentialist (or nineteenth-century) reading of the characters of the sexes, whereas Woolf tends towards the view that any delimitation of the characters of the sexes is itself the problem which her fiction must resolve.

What could permeate, and thus overturn the opposition man/woman – which also involves the opposition woman/woman, since the failure in the first, privileged relationship must prevent ease in the second – is undefined by Mrs Dalloway's meditation. But the discourse of medical science in her day rejected strongly the implications involved in Mrs Dalloway's refusal of a single unitary state, of 'I am this, I am that'. Sexual difference, for Woolf, is founded absolutely on the basis that identity is so delimitable by and within a society. Recent French feminist criticism works from the premise that identities are born through cultural practices, associated with subservience to the rule of patriarchy. Julia Kristeva speaks of the Modernist 'fragmentation' of language, meaning the break-up of solid, realist nineteenth-century narrative-like style. The writing in *Mrs Dalloway* with its breaks and leaps across time and interruptions of the onward flow of events with other moments remembered in metaphor, might be seen as 'fragmented' in that it cuts away from 'a culture where the speaking subjects are conceived of as masters of their speech', as Kristeva puts it. She sees fragmentations as modes of 'traversing or denying' such mastery, adding that 'the word "traverse" implies that the subject experiences sexual difference, not as a fixed opposition ("man"/"woman") but as a process of differentiations'.[9]

'Mastery' in the novel is male-based, or reveals itself in matriarchs whose behaviour borrows from male codes, as when Lady Bexborough shows the same hardness and stoicism that belongs, in mythology, to the battlefield where John died, and which Septimus Smith displayed in relation to the death of Evans. The demand for mastery requires a firm sense of character as self-creation: 'making it up, building it round one' (p. 4), as Peter Walsh creates his Clarissa Dalloway ('For there she was', p. 213). But the novel also suggests that the power to make up the character is still a matter of loss, of misnaming, and that 'the speaking subjects are not masters of their speech' in so creating themselves. Mrs Dalloway discovers this at the mirror, 'seeing the delicate pink face of the woman who was that night to give a party;

of Clarissa Dalloway; of herself. . . . She pursed her lips . . . it was to give her face point. That was her self, pointed, dart-like, definite. That was her self when some effort, some call on her to be her self drew the parts together . . .' (p. 40). The moment in front of the mirror plays on the ambiguity of 'herself' and 'her self', suggests the constructed and partial nature of the self she must create that night, and implies that the peremptory call on Mrs Dalloway to create that self does not allow for individual liberty: it also invokes the subjection of disparate parts so that they can be elided into one unit. An analysis using Kristeva or Lacan would see this naming of the self as dictated by the authority of the law of the Father so that the naming is according to the codes and differences set up within the society that insists on clear-cut differences.

But 'patriarchy' in this novel does not mean something abstract or simply inherent in a family structure: it means the rule of an oppressive state power that has as its spokesmen Bradshaw telling people whether they are well or not in the name of 'Proportion', or Richard Dalloway pronouncing on poetry and on its dangerous emotional or sexual charge. Nor is there anything of abstraction in Woolf's account of the loss the self sustains in its learning of sexual difference. The war-spirit sustains rigid difference and separation. Madness and suicide and coldness imply the price paid for non-recognition of the presence of otherness within the unitary self. Woolf suggests in the news from India, however, that even the Empire cannot be preserved as a monologic and monolithic entity: the signs of otherness are for ever coming back in opposition. The architecture of London, the medical knowledge of the doctors with its power of surveillance, class considerations – registered so potently in people's response to the car going past near the novel's beginning – these elements show how patriarchy as an ideology is created through specific practices within this society. Woolf's stress on veiled homosexuality suggests that what is repressed could either be a source of warmth, if released, or destructive, if not.

Yet though the novel would like to replace the definition and hardness of patriarchalism – the cutting edge of Victorian sculpture giving way to the soft, epiphanic visions of London by Pisarro and Monet, so different from the tastes of the Royal Academy – it might also be said that it can imagine no alternative to the rule of patriarchy. How far, in the end, can it distance itself from Peter Walsh's attitudes?

A splendid achievement in its own way, after all, London; the season; civilisation. Coming as he did from a respectable Anglo-Indian family which for at least three generations had administered the affairs of a continent (it's strange, he thought, what a sentiment I have about that, disliking India, and empire, and army as he did) there were moments when civilisation, even of this sort, seemed dear to him as a personal possession; moments of pride in England; its butlers; chow dogs; girls in their security. . . . And the doctors and men of business and capable women all going about their business, punctual, alert, robust, seemed to him wholly admirable, good fellows, to whom one would entrust one's life . . .

(p. 60)

The ironies here in Walsh's recognition of his own unreasoning sentiments, in the comment on the doctors, in the class-bound choice of things to be noticed for approval, are important. But it is not just the interest in 'the season' that connects Walsh's perceptions to Mrs Dalloway's. He is at home here, as she is, because the status quo suits him very well. The novel's failure, despite its local use of irony, to make something of social as well as sexual difference seems to be the blindness accompanying its insight. The moments when either Mrs Dalloway or Peter Walsh recognise that this London does not suit them can be forgotten as they cannot be for Septimus Smith or Rezia – figures the novel keeps collusively on its margins. Septimus Smith could not really be Mrs Dalloway's double. And neither he nor the others could, after all, attend Mrs Dalloway's party.

From *Essays in Criticism*, 39 (April 1989), 137–55.

NOTES

[Jeremy Tambling reads *Mrs Dalloway* as a novel centrally concerned with history, with the First World War and British imperialism and militarism, and with the possible connections between these things and ideas about the nature of the individual. It uses critical methods deriving from the work of the French thinker Michel Foucault (1926–84), who sought to understand texts in terms of the discourses in which they are constructed, rather than as products of a single authoritative mind and with one overt meaning. Tambling argues that *Mrs Dalloway* criticises the established state as oppressive, and also articulates the modernist idea of personal identity as not fixed but fluid; and that it indicates that rigid definitions of sexual difference are the products of an oppressive society, and that individuals' suffering is frequently the result of such definitions and of the repression of homosexuality. But, he goes on to argue, the novel cannot offer any alternative because it is itself built in the discourses it criticises. It defines its characters in terms of contemporary authoritarian ideas about mental health and illness. It even admires, almost nostalgically, the sophisticated society of a powerful state.

Tambling himself constructs his conclusion in a dominant discourse of today's criticism, describing the opposition within *Mrs Dalloway* in Kristevan or Lacanian terms, as a struggle between the mastery of a dominant narration and the disruption and fragmentation of that narration.

As throughout this volume, references to *Mrs Dalloway* are to the Penguin edition with an Introduction and Notes by Elaine Showalter and text edited by Stella McNichol (London, 1992). Ed.]

1. Leonard Woolf (ed.), *A Writer's Diary. Being Extracts from the Diary of Virginia Woolf* (London and New York, 1953), p. 57: 19 June 1923.

2. The 'Americanisation' of London is discussed by Gavin Weightman and Steve Humphries in *The Making of Modern London 1914–1939* (London, 1984), pp. 9–10 and throughout.

3. See Kate Flint, 'Virginia Woolf and the General Strike', *Essays in Criticism*, 36 (1986), 319–34.

4. David Armstrong, *The Political Anatomy of the Body* (Cambridge, 1983), p. 22.

5. F. R. Leavis, *New Bearings in English Poetry* (London, 1932; Harmondsworth, 1963), p. 84.

6. Paul Fussell, *The Great War and Modern Memory* (Oxford, 1975), ch. 8.

7. Virginia Woolf, *A Room of One's Own* (London, 1929; Penguin edition, 1945, 1992), p. 109.

8. Ibid., p. 97.

9. Julia Kristeva, interview in Elaine Marks and Isabelle de Courtivron (eds), *New French Feminisms* (Brighton, 1981), p. 165.

5

Hume, Stephen, and Elegy in 'To the Lighthouse'

GILLIAN BEER

> When my perceptions are remov'd for any time, as by sound sleep; so long am I insensible of *myself*, and may truly be said not to exist. And were all my perceptions remov'd by death, and cou'd I neither think, nor feel, nor see, nor love, nor hate after the dissolution of my body, I shou'd be entirely annihilated, nor do I conceive what is farther requisite to make me a perfect non-entity.
>
> (David Hume, *A Treatise on Human Nature*)[1]

> Father's birthday. He would have been 96, 96, yes, today; and could have been 96, like other people one has known; but mercifully was not. His life would have entirely ended mine. What would have happened? No writing, no books; – inconceivable. I used to think of him and mother daily; but writing The Lighthouse, laid them in my mind. And now he comes back sometimes, but differently.
>
> (Virginia Woolf, *Diary*, 28 November 1928)[2]

Several of Virginia Woolf's books compose themselves about an absence: Jacob's absence from his room, Mrs Ramsay's in the second half of *To the Lighthouse*, and in *The Waves* Percival's in India and in death. Absence gives predominance to memory and to imagination. Absence may blur the distinction between those who are dead and those who are away. In one sense, everything is absent in fiction, since nothing can be physically there. Fiction blurs the distinction between recall and reading. It creates a form of immediate memory for the reader.

Writing about Hume, the eighteenth-century philosopher he most admired, Leslie Stephen glosses his position thus:

71

The whole history of philosophical thought is but a history of attempts to separate the object and the subject, and each new attempt implies that the previous line of separation was erroneously drawn or partly 'fictitious'.

(p. 48)[3]

In *To the Lighthouse* the fictitiousness of the separation between object and subject, the question of where to draw the line, is passionately explored, not only by the painter, Lily Briscoe, but by the entire narrative process. It is through Lily that the philosophical and artistic problem is most directly expressed and the connection between Mr Ramsay and Hume first mooted. Near the beginning of the book, Lily asks Andrew what his father's books are about.

'Subject and object and the nature of reality,' Andrew had said. And when she said Heavens, she had no notion what that meant. 'Think of a kitchen table then,' he told her, 'when you're not there.'

(p. 28)

In the book's last paragraph, remembering Mrs Ramsay, looking at the empty steps, Lily at last solves the problem of the masses in her picture to her own satisfaction:

She looked at the steps; they were empty; she looked at her canvas; it was blurred. With a sudden intensity, as if she saw it clear for a second, she drew a line there, in the centre.

(p. 226)

The separation of the object and the subject, and the drawing of a line less erroneous, less 'fictitious', than in previous attempts, defines the nature of elegy in this work. Virginia Woolf attempts to honour her obligations to family history and yet freely to dispose that history. In the course of doing so, she brings into question our reliance on symbols to confer value.

Virginia Woolf's other books imply aesthetic theories and draw upon the ideas of contemporary philosophers, particularly Bertrand Russell's warning against assuming that language mirrors the structure of the world: 'Against such errors', he writes in *The Analysis of Mind* (1921), 'the only safeguard is to be able, once in a way, to discard words for a moment and contemplate facts more directly through images.'[4] That is an ideal and a difficulty which moves through

Virginia Woolf's practice as a writer. Only in *To the Lighthouse*, however, is the power of philosophical thinking and its limitations openly a theme of the book. That has to do with the work's special nature as elegy. In 1925, when she was beginning *To the Lighthouse*, Virginia Woolf wrote in her diary:

> I will invent a new name for my books to supplant 'novel': A new —————— by Virginia Woolf. But what? Elegy?

In elegy there is a repetition of mourning and an allaying of mourning. Elegy lets go of the past, formally transferring it into language, laying ghosts by confining them to a text and giving them its freedom. Surviving and relinquishing are both crucial to the composition of *To the Lighthouse*. Learning how to let go may be as deep a difficulty in writing and concluding a novel as it is in other experience.

The problem of achieving and of letting go is shared by mothers and artists. Mrs Ramsay lets go through death. After her death the book continues to explore what lasts (how far indeed has she let go or will others let her go?). The novel questions the means by which we try to hold meaning and make it communicable.

> Meanwhile the mystic, the visionary, walked the beach, stirred a puddle, looked at a stone, and asked themselves 'What am I?' 'What is this?' and suddenly an answer was vouchsafed them (what it was they could not say).
>
> (p. 143)

All Virginia Woolf's novels brood on death, and death, indeed, is essential to their organisation as well as their meaning. Death was her special knowledge: her mother, her sister Stella, and her brother Thoby had all died prematurely. But death was also the special knowledge of her entire generation, through the obliterative experience of the First World War. The long succession of family and generation, so typically the material of the nineteenth-century *roman fleuve*, such as Thackeray's *Pendennis* and *The Virginians*, or Zola's Rougon-Macquart series, becomes the site of disruption. The continuity of the family can with greatest intensity express the problems of invasion and even extinction.

Lawrence originally imagined *The Rainbow* and *Women in Love* as one long novel to be called *The Sisters*. But when the two books eventually appeared the first was a rich genealogical sedimentation,

the second was thinned, lateral, preoccupied with a single generation. The parents in *Women in Love* are enfeebled and dying; the
major relationships explored in the work are chosen, not inherited.
In *To the Lighthouse* Virginia Woolf still tried to hold within a single
work what Lawrence had eventually had to separate: the experience
of family life and culture, before and after the First World War. She
held them together by separating them. 'Time passes', like Lily's line,
both joins and parts. It is one formal expression of the profound
question: 'What endures?' 'Will you fade? Will you perish?', 'The
very stone one kicks with one's boots will outlast Shakespeare'.
'Distant views seem to outlast by a million years (Lily thought) the
gazer and to be communing already with a sky which beholds an
earth entirely at rest.'

> 'Ah, but how long do you think it'll last?' said somebody. It was as if
> she had antennae trembling out of her, which, intercepting certain
> sentences, forced them upon her attention. This was one of them. She
> scented danger for her husband. A question like that would lead,
> almost certainly, to something being said which reminded him of his
> own failure. How long would he be read – he would think at once.
>
> (p. 116)

This passage brings home the other anxiety about survival which
haunts the book: how long will writing last? Mr Ramsay's ambition
to be remembered as a great philosopher registers some of Woolf's
ambitions and longings as an artist too. They are expressed in
another mode by Lily, who must complete her picture and complete
it truly, but who foresees its fate: 'It would be hung in the attics, she
thought; it would be destroyed. But what did that matter? she asked
herself, taking up her brush again' (pp. 225–6). So the topics of the
British empiricists, Locke, Hume, Berkeley – the survival of the
object without a perceiver, the nature of identity and non-entity, the
scepticism about substance – lie beneath the activity of the narrative.
They bear on the question of how we live in our bodies and how we
live in the minds of others. Hume writes of mankind in general that
'they are nothing but a bundle or collection of different perceptions,
which succeed each other with an inconceivable rapidity, and are in
a perpetual flux and movement' (p. 534). The emphasis on perception and on 'flux and movement' is repeated in Virginia Woolf's
writing. But, as I have already suggested, there was a more immediate reason for Hume's insistent and sometimes comic presence in *To
the Lighthouse*.

When Hume is named in *To the Lighthouse* he is strongly identified with Mr Ramsay's thoughts. He is first mentioned at the end of
Mr Ramsay's long meditation on the need for ordinary men and on
their relation to great men (exemplified in the twin figures of Shakespeare and the 'liftman in the Tube'). The section ends with Mr
Ramsay's self-defeated questioning of his own powers. Yet, he thinks:

> he was for the most part happy; he had his wife; he had his children;
> he had promised in six weeks' time to talk 'some nonsense' to the
> young men of Cardiff about Locke, Hume, Berkeley, and the causes of
> the French Revolution.
>
> (p. 51)

His meditation had begun with the question: 'If Shakespeare had
never existed . . . would the world have differed much from what it
is today?' (p. 48). The apposition of empiricism and revolution
('Locke, Hume, Berkeley, and the causes of the French Revolution')
suggests a possible partial answer to that question, but it is self-
deprecatingly framed as 'some nonsense'. The issue remains unresolved.

Hume's name next appears interrupting, and yet almost a part of,
the current of thought generated by Mrs Ramsay in section 11 as she
thinks about 'losing personality', eternity, the lighthouse, and finds
herself repeating phrases: 'Children don't forget. . . . It will end. . . .
It will come. . . . We are in the hands of the Lord.'

> The insincerity slipping in among the truths roused her, annoyed her.
> She returned to her knitting again. How could any Lord have made
> this world? she asked. . . . There was no treachery too base for the
> world to commit; she knew that. No happiness lasted; she knew that.
> She knitted with firm composure, slightly pursing her lips and, without
> being aware of it, so stiffened and composed the lines of her face in a
> habit of sternness that when her husband passed, though he was
> chuckling at the thought that Hume, the philosopher, grown enormously
> fat, had stuck in a bog, he could not help noting, as he passed, the
> sternness at the heart of her beauty.
>
> (p. 71)

Hume, philosopher of mind, has grown so absurdly substantial that
he sinks into the bog. That physical episode becomes meta-memory
for Mr Ramsay, who *sees* it, not having been there. The full story is
reserved for section 13, when at the end:

> the spell was broken. Mr Ramsay felt free now to laugh out loud at

Hume, who had stuck in a bog and an old woman rescued him on condition he said the Lord's Prayer, and chuckling to himself he strolled off to his study.

(p. 80)

Hume, the sceptical philosopher, is obliged to repeat the words of faith. We remember Mrs Ramsay's involuntary 'We are in the hands of the Lord'. Communal faith usurps the individual will. At the end of this episode (section 13) Mr Ramsay feels comfortable: Hume has been worsted. The giant towering above his own endeavours as a philosopher proves to be a gross man subsiding. For a moment he can be held to scale, contained in anecdote. But Mr Ramsay is himself measured by his will to worst. The narrative engages with the difficulties that Hume's work raises. And by this means, as we shall see, Virginia Woolf movingly allows to her father, Leslie Stephen, within her own work, a power of survival, recomposition, rediscovery even.

Hume's presence in the work allows her to bring sharply into focus the question of what is 'when you're not there', a topic traditional to elegy but here given greater acuity. In 1927 Bertrand Russell wrote in *The Analysis of Matter*:

> I believe that matter is less material, and mind less mental, than is commonly supposed, and that, when this is realised, the difficulties raised by Berkeley largely disappear. Some of the difficulties raised by Hume, it is true, have not yet been disposed of.[5]

Hume's persistence, the fact that his difficulties cannot be disposed of, makes him a necessary part of the book's exploration of substance and absence, of writing as survival.

We know that Virginia Woolf read Hume, perhaps not for the first time, in September 1920. But his importance in *To the Lighthouse* is connected with his special value for Leslie Stephen. In the process of transformation from Leslie Stephen to Mr Ramsay, Virginia Woolf notably raises the level of creativity and attainment at which the father-figure is working, placing him in the rearward and yet within reach of major philosophers. Whereas Leslie Stephen was a doughty thinker, high populariser, and man of letters, Mr Ramsay is a possibly major, though self-debilitated, philosopher. This raising and enlarging sustains the scale of the father in relation to the writer and at the same time allows a process of identification between writer and father in their artistic obsessions. Virginia Woolf did not acknowledge having read much of Leslie Stephen's work. But when we turn to Stephen's *History of English Thought in the Eighteenth Century* the congruities between the themes of that work and *To the Lighthouse* are remarkable enough, and Stephen's actual exposition of Hume and the directions in which he seeks to move beyond him are closely related to the concerns of *To the Lighthouse*. The first of these is reputation and survival.

The first sentence of Stephen's book simultaneously places Hume at a pinnacle of achievement and presents the problem of literary reputation.

> Between the years of 1739 and 1752 David Hume published philosophical speculations destined, by the admission of friends and foes, to form a turning-point in the history of thought. His first book fell dead-born from the press; few of its successors had a much better fate.
>
> (p. 1)

The first section of the Introduction is entitled 'The influence of great thinkers' and it grapples with the question of how far the thinker thinks alone or as an expression of communal concerns. How does thought affect society? Stephen argues:

> The soul of the nation was stirred by impulses of which Hume was but one, though by far the ablest, interpreter; or, to speak in less mystical phrase, we must admit that thousands of inferior thinkers were dealing with the same problems which occupied Hume, and though with far less acuteness or logical consistency, arriving at similar conclusions.
>
> (p. 2)

Thinking is not exclusively the province of great thinkers, nor – more strikingly – are their conclusions different from those of others.

In *To the Lighthouse* Mr Bankes suggests:

> We can't all be Titians and we can't all be Darwins, he said: at the same time he doubted whether you could have your Darwin and your Titian if it weren't for humble people like ourselves.
>
> (p. 79)

The relationship between 'humble people like ourselves' – or not quite like ourselves – and great art, great ideas, great events, haunts and troubles *To the Lighthouse*. It is part of the work's deepest questioning of what will survive. The question includes the questioning of the concept of 'great men', of indomitable achievement, of a world centred on human will, and extends to human memory and the material world.

Does the progress of civilisation depend upon great men? Is the lot of the average human being better now than in the time of the pharaohs? Is the lot of the average human being, however, he asked himself, the criterion by which we judge the measure of civilisation? Possibly not. Possibly the greatest good requires the existence of a slave class. The liftman in the Tube is an eternal necessity. The thought was distasteful to him.

(p. 43)

Stephen, pursuing the relationship between 'great men' and the mass of thinking, writes:

Society may thus be radically altered by the influence of opinions which have apparently little bearing upon social questions. It would not be extravagant to say that Mr Darwin's observations upon the breeds of pigeons have had a reaction upon the structure of society.

(p. 12)

Abstract thought and social action seem at times in *To the Lighthouse* to be polarised between Mr and Mrs Ramsay, but most of the thinking in the book is sustained by the activity of laying alongside and intermelding the separate thought processes within individuals in such a way that the reader perceives the connections which the characters themselves cannot. The interpenetration of consciousnesses in language on the page allows us to think through problems of substance and absence unreservedly.

In his analysis of Hume's thought Stephen gives particular emphasis to the idea of fictionality. Stephen writes: 'The belief that anything exists outside our mind when not actually perceived, is a "fiction". . . . Association is in the mental what gravitation is in the natural world.' (Lily's floating table is anchored by association, not gravitation, we remember.)

We can only explain mental processes of any kind by resolving them into such cases of association. Thus reality is to be found only in the ever-varying stream of feelings, bound together by custom, regarded by a 'fiction' or set of fictions as implying some permanent set of external or internal relations. . . . Chance, instead of order, must, it would seem, be the ultimate objective fact, as custom, instead of reason, is the ultimate subjective fact.

(p. 44)

There are obvious connections with *To the Lighthouse* in such an emphasis on reality as an 'ever-varying stream of feelings'. 'Life', he

writes in his discussion of Hume, 'is not entirely occupied in satisfy-
ing our material wants, and co-operating or struggling with our
fellows. We dream as well as act. We must provide some channel for
the emotions generated by contemplation of the world and of ourselves' (p. 11).

Stephen, with Hume, affirms chance and custom rather than order
and reason as the basis of perception. Nevertheless, such affinities
with Virginia Woolf's writing appear at a very general level and need
not imply any particularly intense recall of Stephen's work or conversation. If such consonances were all, I would feel justified only in
calling attention to similarity, rather than implying a process of
rereading, re-placing. However, the actual examples that Stephen
selects are so crucial in the topography of *To the Lighthouse* as to
suggest that Virginia Woolf's writing is meditating on problems
raised in the father's text.

* * *

[Stephen's examples are tree, stone, table and house. The original
essay continues by discussing these points in more detail, in a long
passage which has had to be cut for this volume. Ed.]

To the Lighthouse is a post-symbolist novel. By this I mean that
symbolism is both used and persistently brought into question. The
act of symbolising is one of the major means by which in language
we seek to make things hold, to make them survive. But, above all,
it is the means by which we make *things* serve the human. Symbol
gives primacy to the human because it places the human at the
centre, if not of concern, yet of signifying. Symbol depends for its
nature on the signifying act. By its means concepts and objects are
loaded with human reference.

Though *To the Lighthouse* is weighted with the fullness of human
concerns, there is a constant unrest about the search after a permanence which places humanity at the centre. This search manifests
itself in many ways: as continuity, through generation; as achieved
art object; as storytelling; as memory; as symbol.

Language can never be anything but anthropocentric. In this
book, Virginia Woolf struggles not only with the deaths of her father
and her mother but with the death of that confidence in human
centrality which was already being abraded in her father's generation
by evolutionary theory. When Stephen attempts to move beyond
Hume he does it by means of evolutionist arguments, emphasising
the progressive, the developmental in the theory. The 'race' is Stephen's
new element (and it is an element that Virginia Woolf turns to, much
later, in *Between the Acts*):

> Hume's analysis seems to recognise no difference between the mind of man and a polyp, between the intellectual and the merely sensitive animal . . . the doctrine that belief in the external world is a 'fiction' is apparently self-destructive. If all reason is fiction, fiction is reason.
>
> (p. 49)

> Modern thinkers of Hume's school meet the difficulty by distinguishing between the *a priori* element in the individual mind and in the mind of the race. Each man brings with him certain inherited faculties, if not inherited knowledge; but the faculties have been themselves built up out of the experience of the race.
>
> (p. 56)

Stephen moves away from individualism to a confidence in communal development. *To the Lighthouse* brings into question all such attempts to propose a stable accord between inner and outer, past and present, to seal the contradiction of subject and object through symbol.

> Did Nature supplement what man advanced? Did she complete what he began? With equal complacence she saw his misery, condoned his meanness, and acquiesced in his torture. That dream, then, of sharing, completing, finding in solitude on the beach an answer, was but a reflection in a mirror.
>
> (p. 146)

The signalled anthropomorphism in passages like this ('she saw . . . condoned . . . acquiesced') edges into sight our assumption of equivalence between inner and outer. In the passage describing the house left without people to observe it Virginia Woolf uses a neoclassical personification which strikes oddly, and which is intermelded with animal imagery. 'It is a plain fact of consciousness that we think of a table or house as somehow existing independently of our perception of it', writes Stephen. Here, Virginia Woolf faces the problem of how we describe a house when it exists 'independently of our perception of it'. The answer in 'Time Passes' is to see the object through time, and to use a discourse which points to human absence, sometimes with playful comfort, as in the following passage, sometimes in mourning or ironic abruptness, as in those passages cut off within square brackets '[A shell exploded. Twenty or thirty young men were blown up in France, among them Andrew Ramsay, whose death, mercifully, was instantaneous.]' (p. 145).

> Loveliness and stillness clasped hands in the bedroom, and among the shrouded jugs and sheeted chairs even the prying of the wind, and the soft nose of the clammy sea airs, rubbing, snuffling, iterating, and

reiterating their questions – 'Will you fade? Will you perish?' – scarcely disturbed the peace, the indifference, the air of pure integrity, as if the question they asked scarcely needed that they should answer: we remain.

(p. 141)

The transposed, ludic quality of this passage is part of the decaying humanism of the concept 'house' – an object constructed for human use and so now, without function, present only as lexical play. Beyond the ordinary house is the *lighthouse*, the furthest reach and limit of human concerns, an attempt to create a margin of safety before the sea's power becomes supreme.

The sound of the waves is heard throughout the book, sometimes louder, sometimes softer, but always there to remind us of the expanse of the world beyond the human, in the face of which all attempts at signifying and stabilising are both valiant and absurd. House and table are human objects, made to serve. Can the world of objects be made to sustain our need for signification, continuity, or permanence? These questions, brought to the fore by Hume's scepticism, and struggled with anew in the light of evolutionary theory by Stephen's generation, grind, like the dislimning sea, through *To the Lighthouse*.

The formlessness of the sea and the formed completeness of objects challenge equally the authority of the human subject. 'Subject and Object and the nature of reality' turns out not to be a vapid philosophical trope but the book's grounded enquiry, an enquiry which thrives through her father's concerns.

In generation and in language equally (the making of children and of text) there is an attempt to ward off evanescence. In the course of her novel Virginia Woolf brings these desires within the surveillance of the reader. The tendency of the human to allow predominance to the human, to concur with our sense of our own centrality, is measured. Loading events and objects with symbolic weight comes to be seen as self-gratulation. So, as the work proceeds, she emphasises momentariness and lightness. She empties and thins. The fullness of Part I is replaced by the plainness of Part III. The work is filled with a sense of how ephemeral is human memory: bodies gone and minds with them. All substance is transitory.

In May 1925, as she was beginning *To the Lighthouse*, she wrote in her diary:

This is going to be fairly short: to have father's character done complete in it; and mother's; and St Ives and childhood; and all the usual things

I try to put in – life, death etc. But the centre is father's character, sitting in a boat, reciting We perish, each alone, while he crushes a dying mackerel – However I must refrain.

(III, pp. 18–19)

In the completed work Mrs Ramsay becomes characteristically the centre. The start of Part I, 'The Window', as opposed to Part III, 'The Lighthouse', imitates the self-doubting complexity of Mrs Ramsay's sensibility, a fullness which is resolved later into others' simpler and more ideal memories of her. Certainly much of the emotional and artistic resourcefulness of the work goes into the making again, the repossession, of what the writer too soon had ceased to know: of Vita Sackville-West Virginia Woolf said in December 1925 that she 'lavishes on me the maternal protection which, for some reason, is what I have always most wished from everyone'. But the resourcefulness is also in composing what she could never have known: the meditative consciousness of the mother.

The sexual reserve of the writing is considerable. We never know the first names of Mr or Mrs Ramsay. We do not accompany them to the greenhouses. The distance and decorum do not encourage the same knowingness in the reader as does our pleased recognition that the letter of the alphabet of philosophical knowledge that Mr Ramsay cannot quite reach is that which begins his own name. Yet the Ramsays, the text assertively makes clear, are there when we are not. Their withdrawal emphasises substantiality and sexuality.

All signification relies on memory. In the language of the middle section of 'Time Passes' there is a wilful element, a reclaiming, a making demands, by which the distributor of the language seeks to ward off the immersing sea, the elements, the air, the non-linguistic world of human absence. The assertiveness, stylism, the hyperbole of linguistic desire, have parallels with that haunting figure, Grimm's fisherman's wife, whose story Mrs Ramsay reads to James. And the grossness of the wife's demands has links also with the eagerness of the human to dominate the non-human.

She read on: 'Ah, wife,' said the man, 'why should we be king? I do not want to be king.' Well, said the wife, 'if you won't be king, I will; go to the Flounder, for I will be king.' . . . And when he came to the sea, it was quite dark grey, and the water heaved up from below, and smelt putrid. Then he went and stood by it and said,

'Flounder, flounder, in the sea,
Come, I pray thee, here to me'.

(pp. 62–3)

The last pages of the work void that final claim of the human on the world of process. They pare away symbol. The lighthouse itself when approached proves to be 'a stark tower on a bare rock'. The obsessional symbol-making urge of Mr Ramsay, which is associated with his desire to clutch and hold on to experience, begins to ebb. In the fiction, despite his children's fears, he does *not* say, 'But I beneath a rougher sea' or 'we perished, each alone', though in her diary she projected the scene with him 'sitting in a boat, reciting We perish, each alone, while he crushes a dying mackerel' (*Diary*, III, p. 19). Throughout the book Mr Ramsay has raucously, anxiously, raised his voice against oblivion, terrified by death, and by that longer obliteration in which writing also is lost. But when they reach the place on their journey to the lighthouse where the boat sank in the war (and in 'Time Passes')

> to their surprise all he said was 'Ah' as if he thought to himself, But why make a fuss about that? Naturally men are drowned in a storm, but it is a perfectly straightforward affair, and the depths of the sea (he sprinkled the crumbs from his sandwich paper over them) are only water after all.
>
> (p. 223)

It is a poignant and comic moment. At the moment when highest mystification is expected we are offered a complete demystification. His small gesture, in parenthesis, which recalls and then lets go of the parallel of dust to dust, ashes to ashes, is simply the sprinkling of crumbs on the sea, for the fishes.

That episode is immediately succeeded by another in which symbolism and the mystifying properties of human language and human gesture are relinquished. Lily, thinking their journey, imagines their arrival; '"He has landed," she said aloud. "It is finished."' The last words on the cross are half conjured. Mr Ramsay's journey and agony are momentarily, and uneasily, accorded a scale commensurate with his desires, though one on which, as readers, we are not obliged to dwell. The reference is fleetingly there. But it is immediately succeeded, and submerged, by Lily's finishing of her picture. The last words of the book are:

> With a sudden intensity, as if she saw it clear for a second, she drew a line there, in the centre. It was done; it was finished. Yes, she thought, laying down her brush in extreme fatigue, I have had my vision.

The change of tense, 'It was done; it was finished', obliterates the earlier allusion. The scale of reference becomes immediate, and exact. The step is empty. The picture is finished.

The extraordinary serenity of the book, even while it includes desolation and harassment, depends upon its acceptance of attenuation. Loss, completion, ending, absence, are acknowledged. Evanescence is of the nature of experience, and, although language can for a time make things survive, the work calmly rides out the anxieties of authorship. Though rhyme claims to outlive marble monuments, the pebble survives longer than Shakespeare. But people and language have lived. She renounces the grand, the symbolical, the enduring. The moment is the moment of being alive in body and mind. In her diary in June 1927 she wrote: 'Now one stable moment vanquishes chaos. But this I said in The Lighthouse. We have now sold, I think, 2555 copies' (*Diary*, III, p. 141).

* * *

Lacan argues that symbol and the act of symbolisation represent the father. In freeing characters and text from the appetite for symbol Virginia Woolf may be seen as moving language and persons beyond subjection to patriarchy. And in doing so she transformed and absolved her own father through the act of writing. He comes back, but differently:

> I used to think of him and mother daily; but writing The Lighthouse, laid them in my mind. And now he comes back sometimes, but differently. . . . He comes back now more as a contemporary. I must read him some day. I wonder if I can feel again, I hear his voice, I know this by heart?
>
> (*Diary*, III, p. 208)

A conundrum remains: Virginia Woolf disclaims having 'read' her father. Yet in this essay I have emphasised consonances between their written works. The answer may be that here she purposes a full reading, that act of intimacy, homage, and appraisal in which we subject ourselves to a writer's complete work. She defers any such task, setting it in that warm never-never-land of reading we hope 'some day' to fulfil. The evasion persists. She must delay reading the father. Her earlier familiarity with his work had taken the form of dipping, scanning, listening, a flighty and intrigued resistance which allows rereading and pillaging and avoids immersion.

The wise act of writing in *To the Lighthouse* disperses parenthood and all its symbolic weight. Want and will give way, the want and the will of the fisherman's wife, of Lily Briscoe, of Mrs Ramsay, Mr

Ramsay, of Cam and James. Subject ceases to dominate object. We are left with 'the waves rolling and gambolling and slapping the rocks', 'the frail blue shape which seemed like the vapour of something that had burned itself away', the line in Lily's picture which enters and holds 'all its green and blues, its lines running up and across, its attempt at something'. The line is at last freed from the referential. The picture can be completed.

The end of *To the Lighthouse* performs the experience of ending which has already happened in Mrs Ramsay's reading aloud of Grimm's tale of the fisherman's wife. The end of a story allows annihilation and perpetuity at the same time. Things fall apart and – bring written – for a time, endure.

So Mrs Ramsay equably reads the apocalyptic conclusion to James:

> 'Houses and trees toppled over, the mountains trembled, rocks rolled into the sea, the sky was pitch black, and it thundered and lightened, and the sea came in with black waves as high as church towers and mountains, and all with white foam on top.'
>
> She turned the page; there were only a few lines more, so that she would finish the story, though it was past bedtime. It was getting late. . . . It was growing quite dark.
>
> But she did not let her voice change in the least as she finished the story, and added, shutting the book, and speaking the last words as if she made them up herself, looking into James's eyes: 'And there they are living still at this very time'. 'And that's the end', she said.
>
> (pp. 67–8)

The elegiac triumph of the novel is to sustain entity. People survive when you are not there, when they are not there, in contradiction of Hume's assertion quoted at the beginning of this essay ('were all my perceptions remov'd by death . . . what is farther requisite to make me a perfect non-entity'). But they survive here in a kind of writing which eschews permanence. The last part of the book escapes from symbolic raising, placing its parental figures 'on a level with ordinary existence', with the substance of a chair, a table, a house, with the depths of the sea which (as Mr Ramsay at last thinks) are 'only water after all'.

From Gillian Beer, *Arguing with the Past. Essays in Narrative from Woolf to Sidney* (London, 1989), pp. 183–202.

NOTES

[This essay was first published in 1984 in *Essays in Criticism*, 34, and is one of six essays on Woolf that Gillian Beer has published so far. Professor Beer is concerned to establish the relationships between Woolf's writing and the dominant discourses of her time, both philosophical and historical. Her first four essays, which are all reprinted in *Arguing with the Past* and include this one, read the novels as part of the philosophical enterprise which began with the Victorians' rereading of the past and their struggle with concepts of individualism and determinism. The two more recent essays begin to relate Woolf's fiction to contemporary political and historical experience. 'The Body of the People in Virginia Woolf', in Sue Roe (ed.), *Women Reading Women Writing* (1987), argues that Woolf is as interested in communities of people as in private consciousness, and cites *Mrs Dalloway*'s examination of different people all present on the same day in London. 'The Island and the Aeroplane: the Case of Virginia Woolf', in Homi Bhabha (ed.), *Nation and Narration* (1990), which includes fascinating close readings of the passages about aeroplanes in *Mrs Dalloway* and other Woolf novels, takes Woolf's work as an indicative example of how ideas of national identity in British writing are changing.

The essay in part reprinted here approaches *To the Lighthouse* through Woolf's own statements connecting it with her father, and discovers in it a careful debate with Leslie Stephen's writing. Read this way, *To the Lighthouse* becomes both Woolf's personal exorcism of her memories of her parents, and a philosophical exploration of old ideas about objective existence and of newer ideas about language's function as the creator of meaning.

As throughout this volume, references to *To the Lighthouse* are to the Penguin edition with Introduction and Notes by Hermione Lee and text edited by Stella McNichol (London, 1992). Ed.]

1. David Hume, *A Treatise on Human Nature* (1736), ed. T. H. Green and T. H. Gross (London, 1874), vol. 1, p. 534. All further references are to this edition and appear in the text in parentheses.

2. Anne Olivier Bell (ed.), *The Diary of Virginia Woolf*, vol. 3 (London, 1980), p. 208. Further page references appear in the text in parentheses.

3. Leslie Stephen, *English Thought in the Eighteenth Century*, 2 vols (London, 1876). Page references appear in the text in parentheses.

4. For discussion of this topic, see Allen McLaurin, *Virginia Woolf: The Echoes Enslaved* (Cambridge, 1973).

5. Bertrand Russell, *The Analysis of Matter* (London, 1927), p. 7.

6

Who's Afraid of Virginia Woolf? Feminist Readings of Woolf

TORIL MOI

Woolf seems to practise what we might now call a 'deconstructive' form of writing, one that engages with and thereby exposes the duplicitous nature of discourse. In her own textual practice, Woolf exposes the way in which language refuses to be pinned down to an underlying essential meaning. According to the French philosopher Jacques Derrida, language is structured as an endless deferral of meaning, and any search for an essential, absolutely stable meaning must therefore be considered metaphysical. There is no final element, no fundamental unit, no *transcendental signified* that is meaningful *in itself* and thus escapes the ceaseless interplay of linguistic deferral and difference. The free play of signifiers will never yield a final, unified meaning that in turn might ground and explain all the others.[1] It is in the light of such textual and linguistic theory that we can read Woolf's playful shifts and changes of perspective, in both her fiction and in *Room*, as something rather more than a wilful desire to irritate the serious-minded feminist critic. Through her conscious exploitation of the sportive, sensual nature of language, Woolf rejects the metaphysical essentialism underlying patriarchal ideology, which hails God, the Father or the phallus as its transcendental signified.

But Woolf does more than practise a non-essentialist form of writing. She also reveals a deeply sceptical attitude to the male-humanist concept of an essential human identity. For what can this self-identical identity be if all meaning is a ceaseless play of difference, if *absence* as much as presence is the foundation of meaning? The humanist concept of identity is also challenged by psychoanalytic theory, which Woolf undoubtedly knew. The Hogarth Press, founded by Virginia and Leonard Woolf, published the first English translations of Freud's central works, and when Freud arrived in London in 1939 Virginia Woolf went to visit him. Freud, we are tantalisingly informed, gave her a narcissus.

For Woolf, as for Freud, unconscious drives and desires constantly exert a pressure on our conscious thoughts and actions. For psychoanalysis the human subject is a complex entity, of which the conscious mind is only a small part. Once one has accepted this view of the subject, however, it becomes impossible to argue that even our conscious wishes and feelings originate within a unified self, since we can have no knowledge of the possibly unlimited unconscious processes that shape our conscious thought. Conscious thought, then, must be seen as the 'overdetermined' manifestation of a multiplicity of structures that intersect to produce that unstable constellation the liberal humanists call the 'self'. These structures encompass not only unconscious sexual desires, fears and phobias, but also a host of conflicting material, social, political and ideological factors of which we are equally unaware. It is this highly complex network of conflicting structures, the anti-humanist would argue, that produces the subject and its experiences, rather than the other way round. This belief does not of course render the individual's experiences in any sense less real or valuable; but it does mean that such experiences cannot be understood other than through the study of their multiple determinants – determinants of which conscious thought is only one, and a potentially treacherous one at that. If a similar approach is taken to the literary text, it follows that the search for a unified individual self, or gender identity or indeed 'textual identity' in the literary work must be seen as drastically reductive.

It is in this sense that Elaine Showalter's recommendation to remain detached from the narrative strategies of the text is equivalent to not reading it at all. For it is only through an examination of the detailed strategies of the text on all its levels that we will be able to uncover some of the conflicting, contradictory elements that contribute to make it precisely *this* text, with precisely these words and this configuration. The humanist desire for a unity of vision or thought (or as Holly puts it, for a 'noncontradictory perception of the world'[2])

is, in effect, a demand for a sharply reductive reading of literature –
a reading that, not least in the case of an experimental writer like
Woolf, can have little hope of grasping the central problems posed by
pioneering modes of textual production. A 'non-contradictory perception of the world', for Lukács's Marxist opponent Bertolt Brecht,
is precisely a reactionary one.

The French feminist philosopher Julia Kristeva has argued that the
modernist poetry of Lautréamont, Mallarmé and others constitutes a
'revolutionary' form of writing. The modernist poem, with its abrupt
shifts, ellipses, breaks and apparent lack of logical construction is a
kind of writing in which the rhythms of the body and the unconscious have managed to break through the strict rational defences of
conventional social meaning. Since Kristeva sees such conventional
meaning as the structure that sustains the whole of the symbolic
order – that is, all human social and cultural institutions – the
fragmentation of symbolic language in modernist poetry comes for
her to parallel and prefigure a total *social* revolution. For Kristeva,
that is to say, there is a *specific practice of writing* that is itself
'revolutionary', analogous to sexual and political transformation,
and that by its very existence testifies to the possibility of transform-
ing the symbolic order of orthodox society from the inside.[3] One
might argue in this light that Woolf's refusal to commit herself in her
essays to a so-called rational or logical form of writing, free from
fictional techniques, indicates a similar break with symbolic language, as of course do many of the techniques she deploys in her
novels.

Kristeva also argues that many women will be able to let what she
calls the 'spasmodic force' of the unconscious disrupt their language
because of their strong links with the pre-Oedipal mother-figure. But
if those unconscious pulsations were to take over the subject entirely,
the subject would fall back into pre-Oedipal or imaginary chaos and
develop some form of mental illness. The subject whose language lets
such forces disrupt the symbolic order, in other words, is also the
subject who runs the greater risk of lapsing into madness. Seen in this
context, Woolf's own periodic attacks of mental illness can be linked
both to her textual strategies and to her feminism. For the symbolic
order is a patriarchal order, ruled by the Law of the Father, and any
subject who tries to disrupt it, who lets unconscious forces slip
through the symbolic repression, puts her or himself in a position of
revolt against this regime. Woolf herself suffered acute patriarchal
oppression at the hands of the psychiatric establishment, and *Mrs*

Dalloway contains not only a splendidly satirical attack on that profession (as represented by Sir William Bradshaw), but also a superbly perspicacious representation of a mind that succumbs to 'imaginary' chaos in the character of Septimus Smith. Indeed Septimus can be seen as the negative parallel to Clarissa Dalloway, who herself steers clear of the threatening gulf of madness only at the price of repressing her passions and desires, becoming a cold but brilliant woman highly admired in patriarchal society. In this way Woolf discloses the dangers of the invasion of unconscious pulsions as well as the price paid by the subject who successfully preserves her sanity, thus maintaining a precarious balance between an overestimation of so-called 'feminine' madness and a too precipitate rejection of the values of the symbolic order.

It is evident that for Julia Kristeva it is not the biological sex of a person, but the subject position she or he takes up, that determines their revolutionary potential. Her views of feminist politics reflect this refusal of biologism and essentialism. The feminist struggle, she argues, must be seen historically and politically as a three-tiered one, which can be schematically summarised as follows:

1 Women demand equal access to the symbolic order. Liberal feminism. Equality.
2 Women reject the male symbolic order in the name of differ- ence. Radical feminism. Femininity extolled.
3 (This is Kristeva's own position.) Women reject the dichotomy between masculine and feminine as metaphysical.

The third position is one that has deconstructed the opposition between masculinity and femininity, and therefore necessarily chal- lenges the very notion of identity. Kristeva writes:

> In the third attitude, which I strongly advocate – which I imagine? – the very dichotomy man/woman as an opposition between two rival entities may be understood as belonging to *metaphysics*. What can 'identity', even 'sexual identity', mean in a new theoretical and scientific space where the very notion of identity is challenged?[4]

The relationship between the second and the third positions here requires some comment. If the defence of the third position implies a total rejection of stage two (which I do not think it does), this would be a grievous political error. For it still remains *politically* essential for feminists to defend women *as* women in order to counteract the patriarchal oppression that precisely despises women *as* women. But an 'undeconstructed' form of 'stage two' feminism, unaware of the metaphysical nature of gender identities, runs the risk of becoming an inverted form of sexism. It does so by uncritically taking over the very metaphysical categories set up by patriarchy in order to keep women in their places, despite attempts to attach new feminist values to these old categories. An adoption of Kristeva's 'deconstructed' form of feminism therefore in one sense leaves everything as it was – our positions in the political struggle have not changed – but in another sense radically transforms our awareness of the nature of that struggle.

Here, I feel, Kristeva's feminism echoes the position taken up by Virginia Woolf some sixty years earlier. Read from this perspective, *To the Lighthouse* illustrates the destructive nature of a metaphysical belief in strong, immutably fixed gender identities – as represented by Mr and Mrs Ramsay – whereas Lily Briscoe (an artist) represents the subject who deconstructs this opposition, perceives its pernicious influence and tries as far as is possible in a still rigidly patriarchal order to live as her own woman, without regard for the crippling definitions of sexual identity to which society would have her conform. It is in this context that we must situate Woolf's crucial concept of androgyny. This is not, as Showalter argues, a flight from fixed gender identities, but a recognition of their falsifying metaphysical nature. Far from fleeing such gender identities because she fears them, Woolf rejects them because she has seen them for what they are. She has understood that the goal of the feminist struggle must precisely be to deconstruct the death-dealing binary oppositions of masculinity and femininity.

In her fascinating book *Toward Androgyny*, published in 1973, Carolyn Heilbrun sets out her own definition of androgyny in similar terms when she describes it as the concept of an 'unbounded and hence fundamentally indefinable nature'.[5] When she later finds it necessary to distinguish androgyny from feminism, and therefore implicitly defines Woolf as a non-feminist, her distinction seems to be based on the belief that only the first two stages of Kristeva's three-tiered struggle could count as feminist strategies. She acknowledges that in modern-day society it might be difficult to separate the defenders of androgyny from feminists, 'because of the power men now hold, and because of the political weakness of women'[6] but refuses to draw the conclusion that feminists can in fact desire androgyny. As opposed to Heilbrun, I would stress with Kristeva that a theory that demands the deconstruction of sexual identity is indeed authentically feminist. In Woolf's case the question is rather whether or not her remarkably advanced understanding of feminist objectives prevented her from taking up a progressive political position in the feminist struggles of her day. In the light of *Three Guineas* (and of *A Room of One's Own*), the answer to this question is surely no. The Woolf of *Three Guineas* shows an acute awareness of the dangers of both liberal and radical feminism (Kristeva's positions one and two), and argues instead for a 'stage three' position; but despite her objections she ends up firmly in favour of women's right to financial independence, education and entry into the professions – all central issues for feminists of the 1920s and 1930s.

Nancy Topping Bazin reads Woolf's concept of androgyny as the *union* of masculinity and femininity – precisely the opposite, in fact, of viewing it as the deconstruction of the duality. For Bazin, masculinity and femininity in Woolf are concepts that retain their full essential charge of meaning. She thus argues that Lily Briscoe in *To the Lighthouse* must be read as being just as feminine as Mrs Ramsay, and that the androgynous solution of the novel consists in a *balance* of the masculine and the feminine 'approach to truth'.[7] Herbert Marder, conversely, advances in his *Feminism and Art* the trite and traditional case that Mrs Ramsay must be seen as an androgynous ideal in herself: 'Mrs Ramsay as wife, mother, hostess, is the androgynous artist in life, creating with the whole of her being'.[8] Heilbrun rightly rejects such a reading, claiming that:

> It is only in groping our way through the clouds of sentiment and misplaced biographical information that we are able to discover Mrs Ramsay, far from androgynous and complete, to be as one-sided and life-denying as her husband.[9]

The host of critics who with Marder read Mrs Ramsay and Mrs Dalloway as Woolf's ideal of femininity are thus either betraying their vestigial sexism – the sexes are fundamentally different and should stay that way – or their adherence to what Kristeva would call a 'stage two' feminism: women are different from men and it is time they began praising the superiority of their sex. These are both, I believe, misreadings of Woolf's texts, as when Kate Millett writes that:

> Virginia Woolf glorified two housewives, Mrs Dalloway and Mrs Ramsay, recorded the suicidal misery of Rhoda in *The Waves* without

ever explaining its causes, and was argumentative yet somehow unsuccessful, perhaps because unconvinced, in conveying the frustrations of the woman artist in Lily Briscoe.[10]

A combination of Derridean and Kristevan theory, then, would seem to hold considerable promise for future feminist readings of Woolf. But it is important to be aware of the political limitations of Kristeva's arguments. Though her views on the 'politics of the subject' constitute a significant contribution to revolutionary theory, her belief that the revolution within the subject somehow prefigures a later social revolution poses severe problems for any materialist analysis of society. The strength of Kristevan theory lies in its emphasis on the politics of language as a material and social structure, but it takes little or no account of other conflicting ideological and material structures that must be part of any radical social transformation. It should nevertheless be emphasised that the 'solution' to Kristeva's problems lies not in a speedy return to Lukács, but in an integration and transvaluation of her ideas within a larger feminist theory of ideology.[11]

A Marxist-feminist critic like Michèle Barrett has stressed the materialist aspect of Woolf's politics. In her introduction to *Virginia Woolf: Women and Writing*, she argues that:

> Virginia Woolf's critical essays offer us an unparalleled account of the development of women's writing, perceptive discussion of her predecessors and contemporaries, and a pertinent insistence on the material conditions which have structured women's consciousness.[12]

Barrett, however, considers Woolf only as essayist and critic, and seems to take the view that when it comes to her fiction, Woolf's aesthetic theory, particularly the concept of an androgynous art, 'continually resists the implications of the materialist position she advances in *A Room of One's Own*' (p. 22). A Kristevan approach to Woolf, as I have argued, would refuse to accept this binary opposition of aesthetics on the one hand and politics on the other, locating the politics of Woolf's writing *precisely in her textual practice*. That practice is of course much more marked in the novels than in most of the essays.

Another group of feminist critics, centred around Jane Marcus, consistently argue for a radical reading of Woolf's work without recourse to either Marxist or poststructuralist theory. Jane Marcus claims Woolf as a 'guerrilla fighter in a Victorian skirt',[13] and sees in her a champion of both socialism and feminism. Marcus's article

'Thinking back through our mothers', however, makes it abundantly clear that it is exceptionally difficult to argue this case convincingly. Her article opens with this assertion:

> Writing, for Virginia Woolf, was a revolutionary act. Her alienation from British patriarchal culture and its capitalist and imperialist forms and values, was so intense that she was filled with terror and determination as she wrote. A guerrilla fighter in a Victorian skirt, she trembled with fear as she prepared her attacks, her raids on the enemy.[14]

Are we to believe that there is a causal link between the first and the following sentences – that writing was a revolutionary act for Woolf *because* she could be seen to tremble as she wrote? Or should the passage be read as an extended metaphor, as an image of the fears of *any* woman writing under patriarchy? In which case it no longer tells us anything specific about Woolf's particular writing practices. Or again, perhaps the first sentence is the claim that the following sentences are meant to corroborate? If this is the case, the argument also fails. For Marcus here unproblematically evokes biographical evidence to sustain her thesis about the nature of Woolf's writing: the reader is to be convinced by appeals to biographical circumstances rather than to the texts. But does it really matter whether or not Woolf was in the habit of trembling at her desk? Surely what matters is what she wrote? This kind of emotionalist argument surfaces again in Marcus's extensive discussion of the alleged parallels between Woolf and the German Marxist critic Walter Benjamin ('Both Woolf and Benjamin chose suicide rather than exile before the tyranny of fascism'[15]). But surely Benjamin's suicide at the Spanish frontier, where as an exiled German Jew fleeing the Nazi occupation of France he feared being handed over to the Gestapo, must be considered in a rather different light from Woolf's suicide in her own back garden in unoccupied England, however political we might wish her private life to be? Marcus's biographical analogies strive to establish Woolf as a remarkable individual, and so fall back into the old-style historical-biographical criticism much in vogue before the American New Critics entered the scene in the 1930s. How far a radical feminist approach can simply take over such traditional methods untransformed is surely debatable.

We have seen that current Anglo-American feminist criticism tends to read Woolf through traditional aesthetic categories, relying largely on a liberal-humanist version of the Lukácsian aesthetics, against which Brecht so effectively polemicised. The anti-humanist reading I have advocated as yielding a better understanding of the political nature of Woolf's aesthetics has yet to be written. The only study of Woolf to have integrated some of the theoretical advances of poststructuralist thought is written by a man, Perry Meisel, and though it is by no means an anti-feminist or even an unfeminist work, it is nevertheless primarily concerned with the influence on Woolf of Walter Pater. Meisel is the only critic of my acquaintance to have gasped the radically deconstructed character of Woolf's texts:

> With 'difference' the reigning principle in Woolf as well as Pater, there can be no natural or inherent characteristics of any kind, even between the sexes, because all character, all language, even the language of sexuality, emerges by means of a difference from itself.[16]

Meisel also shrewdly points out that this principle of difference makes it impossible to select any one of Woolf's works as more representative, more essentially 'Woolfian' than any other, since the notable divergence among her texts 'forbids us to believe any moment in Woolf's career to be more conclusive than another'. It is a mistake, Meisel concludes, to 'insist on the coherence of self and author in the face of a discourse that dislocates or decentres them both, that skews the very categories to which our remarks properly refer'.[17]

The paradoxical conclusion of our investigations into the feminist reception of Woolf is therefore that she has yet to be adequately welcomed and acclaimed by her feminist daughters in England and America. To date she has either been rejected by them as insufficiently feminist, or praised on grounds that seem to exclude her fiction. By their more or less unwitting subscription to the humanist aesthetic categories of the traditional male academic hierarchy, feminist critics have seriously undermined the impact of their challenge to that very institution. The only difference between a feminist and a non-feminist critic in this tradition then becomes the formal political perspective of the critic. The feminist critic thus unwittingly puts herself in a position from which it becomes impossible to read Virginia Woolf as the progressive, feminist writer of genius she undoubtedly was. A feminist criticism that would do both justice and homage to its great mother and sister: this, surely, should be our goal.

From Toril Moi, *Sexual/Textual Politics: Feminist Literary Theory*
(London and New York, 1985), pp. 9–18.

NOTES

[Toril Moi's *Sexual/Textual Politics: Feminist Literary Theory* made a wide
range of readers and students aware that the work of Hélène Cixous, Luce
Irigaray, and, especially, Julia Kristeva might be directly related to the
reading of other texts. The essay printed here is most of the second half of
Moi's Introduction. In the first half Moi laments the lack of admiration
accorded, at her time of writing, by feminist critics to Woolf, whom she calls
'this great feminist writer' (*Sexual/Textual Politics*, p. 2) and 'the greatest
British woman writer of this century' (p. 8). She argues that critics such as
Elaine Showalter, whose influential *A Literature of Their Own* (1977) had
accused Woolf of failing to present readers with a strong representation of
her suffering as a woman, are making naïve demands of Woolf's texts. With
Showalter's work she specifically groups Patricia Stubbs's *Women and Fiction. Feminism and the Novel 1880–1920* (Brighton, 1981) and Marcia
Holly's essay 'Consciousness and Authenticity: Toward a Feminist Aesthetic'
(1975) (see note 2 below). Comparing these three with the Marxist critic
Georg Lukács (see note 9 below), Moi argues that they work from the
'humanist' belief that individuals are fixed entities who have defined experiences which can be objectively observed; and that they simplistically demand
that women's writing should give an 'authentic' and realistic account of
women's observed experience.

  In the second part of her Introduction, reprinted here, Moi opposes this
idea of the individual to that of the French theorists. Here she argues that
consciousness is fluid, and constructed by forces of which the individual is
unaware. She proposes a way of reading that sees the text as a place in which
consciousness is enacted, not as a representation of objective experience; and
argues that Woolf's writing must be read in this way. Ed.]

1. [In her original note Moi refers readers, for an introduction to Derrida's
   thought and to other forms of deconstruction, to Christopher Norris,
   Deconstruction: Theory and Practice (London and New York, 1982).
   Ed.]

2. [Moi is referring to Marcia Holly, 'Consciousness and Authenticity:
   Toward a Feminist Aesthetic', in Josephine Donovan (ed.), *Feminist
   Literary Criticism. Explorations in Theory* (Lexington, 1975), pp. 38–
   47). Ed.]

3. [Moi writes, in a note to the original essay, that this presentation of
   Kristeva's position is based on her *La Révolution du langage poétique*
   (Paris, 1974). Selections from this, in translation, appear in Toril Moi
   (ed.), *The Kristeva Reader* (Oxford, 1986), pp. 89–136. Ed.]

4. [This quotation is from Kristeva's essay 'Le Temps des Femmes' (Paris, 1979), translated as 'Women's Time' in Toril Moi (ed.), *The Kristeva Reader*, p. 209. Ed.]

5. Carolyn G. Heilbrun, *Toward Androgyny. Aspects of Male and Female in Literature* (London, 1973), p. xi.

6. Ibid., pp. xvi–xvii.

7. Nancy Topping Bazin, *Virginia Woolf and the Androgynous Vision* (New Brunswick NJ, 1973), p. 138.

8. Herbert Marder, *Feminism and Art. A Study of Virginia Woolf* (Chicago and London, 1968), p. 128.

9. *Toward Androgyny*, p. 155.

10. Kate Millett, *Sexual Politics* (1969; London, 1977), pp. 139–40.

11. [In the earlier part of the Introduction (*Sexual/Textual Politics*, pp. 4–6) Moi compared Showalter's demand for 'a powerful expression of personal experience in a social framework' in feminist writing with the 'proletarian humanism' of Lukács. Of Lukács's work she particularly cites, in a note, his 'Preface' in *Studies in European Realism. A Sociological Survey of the Writings of Balzac, Stendhal, Zola, Tolstoy, Gorki and Others* (London, 1972), pp. 1–19. Ed.]

12. Michèle Barrett (ed.), *Virginia Woolf: Women and Writing* (London, 1979), p. 36.

13. Jane Marcus (ed.), *New Feminist Essays on Virginia Woolf* (Nebraska and London, 1981), p. 1.

14. Ibid., p. 1.

15. Ibid., p. 7.

16. Perry Meisel, *The Absent Father. Virginia Woolf and Walter Pater* (New Haven, 1980), p. 234.

17. Ibid., p. 242.

7

'Mrs Dalloway'

MAKIKO MINOW-PINKNEY

The problem for woman is to assert a female specificity as difference and to open up a space for this difference in the masculine structure of society. This is not to be achieved simply by the assertion of women's comradeship; it involves, rather, the question of the subject. Having remained close to the maternal body in spite of its enforced repression, the girl or woman inscribes herself naturally within the semiotic, in touch with what Kristeva terms the 'spasmodic force' of the repressed. Her task is then to affirm this force, to find the practices appropriate to it, but this is not a matter of its defining a separate, substantive symbolic of its own. It will rather at best be enacted as a moment *inherent* in the rejection of the process of the ruptures, of the rhythmic breaks. Kristeva writes: 'Insofar as she has a specificity of her own, a woman finds it in asociality, in the violation of communal conventions, in a sort of a-symbolic singularity'.[1] Menaced equally by the paternal paranoia and the mother's schizophrenia, the daughter must maintain herself in a difficult equilibrium between the two.

Women must somehow keep a hold on the symbolic, and thus as if in reinforcement of the mirror phase – the threshold of formation of the unitary ego – Clarissa needs her own reflection: 'the delicate pink face of the woman . . . of Clarissa Dalloway; of herself' (p. 40). She 'assembles' the self 'when some effort, some call on her self' constrains her, and then becomes conscious of the lack of 'something central which permeated' (p. 34). This lack is the maternal body which she must repress to become a subject in the symbolic. Because of this denial of the maternal and her own body, 'there was an

emptiness about the heart of life; an attic room' to which she aus-
terely withdraws 'like a nun' (p. 33). Sally, who more fully owns her
body, is quick to detect this absence in Clarissa: 'But – did Peter
understand? – she lacked something' (p. 207). The novel stresses this
withdrawal from the body in several ways. Clarissa had 'grown very
white since her illness'. She is the mere ghost of a woman, cut away
by physical infirmity from the energies of bodily life. There is,
moreover, 'a touch of the bird about her, of the jay, blue-green, light
vivacious' (p. 4). Such energy as she retains is light and ethereal,
more spiritual than physical. And, finally, she is in her fifties, cut off
by the fact of menopause from the fertile biological processes of
ovulation and menstruation.

The most positive representative of the body in the novel is the
younger Sally Seton, who 'forgot her sponge, and ran along the
passage naked' (p. 37). Sally's fascination for Clarissa is 'a sort of
abandonment', that is, her different relationship to her own body.
Sally teaches Clarissa about sex, speaks of sexual matters in front of
men, shocks others by running along the passage naked. She confidently asserts herself as a woman, 'as if she could say anything, do
anything' (p. 35). Not that her feminist boldness goes altogether
unpunished. Hugh Whitbread's kiss is an act of sexual violence, the
rape on a miniature scale of a woman who has dared argue that her
sex should have the vote. But to our and Clarissa's disappointment
the apparently fearless Sally has married a capitalist millionaire and
now has five sons. Maternity is the only female identity which is
valorised by patriarchy. Only as a mother is a woman allowed to
have her sexuality as difference, to own her body and social place.
The novel's arch-rebel becomes a sober conformist, 'Lady Rossiter'.

Repressing the body, Clarissa is given a place in the symbolic
order constructed around the Name-of-the-Father:

> this body, with all its capacities, seemed nothing – nothing at all. She
> had the oddest sense of being herself invisible; unseen; unknown; there
> being no more marrying, no more having of children now, but only
> this astonishing and rather solemn progress with the rest of them, up
> Bond Street, this being Mrs Dalloway; not even Clarissa any more; this
> being Mrs Richard Dalloway.
>
> (p. 11)

'Not even Clarissa': once subdued to the laws of the father, a woman
is next handed over to another man, the husband, as commodity in
the structure of patriarchal exchange relations. Throughout the novel

Clarissa's mother is curiously repressed, though her father is always prominent in her memories. Only once, at the party, does a guest exclaim that Clarissa looks that night 'so like her mother': 'And really Clarissa's eyes filled with tears', but this brief 'return' of her mother is instantly cancelled by her duty as hostess of patriarchy (p. 193). This repression of the mother is also a denial of the maternal in herself, 'unmaternal as she was' (p. 209). Women have to be the daughters of their fathers, not their mothers. Childbirth can no more rupture her hymen outwards than the phallus could inwards; she retains 'a virginity preserved through childbirth' (p. 34). She cannot move from girlhood to full womanhood, and is constantly defensive about her own maternity. Even Walsh notices the over-emphasis with which she declares 'Here is my Elizabeth' (p. 52), and later concludes that the daughter probably does not get on with her mother. Seeing Clarissa, Walsh notes that women attach themselves to places; and their fathers – a woman's always proud of her father' (p. 60). In 'Mrs Dalloway in Bond Street' Clarissa recalls 'A happy childhood – and it was not to his daughters only that Justin Parry had seemed a fine fellow'.[2] Breaking away from the mother, Clarissa accepts the role prescribed by the paternal law, becoming 'the perfect hostess' (p. 8). And this repudiation of the mother is repeated in Elizabeth; Sally could 'feel it by the way Elizabeth went to her father' (p. 212).

The pain of severance from the maternal generates in the subject for the rest of its life a desire for its overcoming, but the risk of fusing with the mother is shown in Peter's dream in Regent's Park. He falls asleep beside an elderly nurse who 'resumed her knitting' as he began snoring. Here is a female knitter more reassuring than the formidable Clarissa–Penelope. Peter's dream of the solitary traveller evokes some ultimate principle of womanliness which will 'shower down from her magnificent hands, compassion, comprehension, absolution' (p. 63). Walsh had found himself repelled by the 'coldness' and 'impenetrability' of Clarissa, and therefore thinks 'rather let me walk straight on to this great figure, who will, with a toss of her head, mount me on her streamers and let me blow to nothingness with the rest' (p. 63). Fusion with the maternal is thus an instant dispersal of the human subject. But the passage is deeply ambivalent because the novel recognises that Peter is invoking an ideology of femininity in order to avoid contact with the *real* woman. Hence it speaks of 'the visions which ceaselessly float up, pace beside, put their faces in front of, the actual thing' (p. 63), and hence the satirical tone, as when the Sirens are 'lolloping away on the green sea waves' (p. 62). Yet even this ideological stereotype of the feminine does answer to certain deep-seated needs of the subject, and the sea imagery relates to those more utopian visions of the sea as a great pulsing semiotic *chora* which I discussed earlier.[3]

The voice of the 'battered woman' singing opposite the tube station is precisely the voice of the mother, issuing from 'a mere hole in the earth' (p. 89). The woman or mother is always a void, a hole in discourse – as the unconscious, the unrepresentable: 'so rude a mouth, a mere hole in the earth, muddy too, matted with root fibres and tangled grasses', an image irresistibly suggesting the female genitals. This singing voice 'bubbles up without direction, vigour, beginning or end' and 'with an absence of all human meaning into ee um fah um so/foo swee too eem oo' (pp. 88–9). A mere rhythmic babble of phonemes, this 'old bubbling, burbling song' of the pre-symbolic becomes something like the very energy behind evolution. It has endured 'through all ages – when the pavement was grass, when it was swamp, through the age of tusk and mammoth' (p. 89). The ancient woman offers an alternative, 'feminist' view of evolution to set against the patriarchal social Darwinism of Sir William Bradshaw, whereby only the fittest or those with a 'sense of proportion' survive.

Just as the broken syllables of the old woman's song escape the lexical and syntactic grids of the symbolic order, so she has no place within society but wanders freely as a tramp. Clarissa, in contrast, is 'a perfect hostess'. But this complicity with patriarchy arouses an intense hostility in Miss Kilman, who has been 'cheated' by the male social order (p. 135). Kilman is a 'phallic woman', who identifies with the Father, denying her femaleness and 'becoming' a man herself.[4] Hence Clarissa can only conceive of Kilman's hated existence as a phallic scraping of delicate interior membranes: 'It rasped her, though, to have stirring about in her this brutal monster . . . had the power to make her feel scraped, hurt in her spine; gave her physical pain' (p. 13). Kilman does not 'dress to please', and hates Clarissa's feminine delicacy and fashionableness – 'the most worthless of all classes' (p. 135). But because of her inferior class-position, Kilman has had to adopt the most aggressive masculine values to secure a niche for herself. She is dominated by the male spirit of 'conversion' and even her love for Elizabeth becomes a rapacious desire for possession. In attempting to conform to the mores of male society, Kilman has had to repress the maternal and the body, just as Clarissa did.

'It was the flesh that she must control' (p. 140). She must subjugate 'her unlovable body', and desperately resorts to religion, 'for the light in the Abbey was bodiless' (p. 146). It is her superabundant physicality – 'her largeness, robustness and power' (p. 147) – that strikes people, taking the form of a powerful *smell* about which the novel remains coy. At tea, Elizabeth reflects that 'it was rather stuffy in here' and when she gets out finds 'the fresh air so delicious' (pp. 144–9). Earlier Clarissa thinks of Kilman 'mewed in a stuffy bedroom' (p. 12), and when she reflects that 'year in year out she wore that coat: she perspired; she was never in the room five minutes without making you feel her superiority', this final noun is not quite what we had been expecting! It is precisely the effort to repress the body that turns it sour and rancid, for Kilman's disgusting odour is in stark contrast to the healthy smell of Richard Dalloway: 'when he came into the room he smelt of stables' (p. 207). The heavy stress on Kilman's perspiration reveals her as a principle of heat in contrast to Clarissa as the principle of ice and austerity, and this may lend another meaning to Clarissa's desire to 'fear no more the heat o' the sun'.

'With all this luxury going on, what hope was there for a better state of things? Instead of lying on a sofa . . . she should have been in a factory' (p. 136). Kilman's denunciation of Clarissa is perfectly justified, and Peter similarly criticises her indolent life-style. By making Kilman so distastefully aggressive, however, the novel encourages us to discount her attack on Clarissa's complicity with the patriarchy, the contradiction that she depends on an imperialistic society to afford the material conditions for the possibility of values – 'the privacy of the soul' (p. 139) – which that society at the same time negates. This is the very contradiction that Raymond Williams has noted of Bloomsbury in general: that the Bloomsbury intellectuals were culturally superior to and contemptuous of the bourgeoisie to whom they were mere administrative functionaries.[5] Clarissa's distant attitude to Sally's husband as self-made capitalist further attests this distaste for the bourgeoisie, as does the novel's hostility to Sir William Bradshaw as a member of the ideological thought-police of the capitalist order. Bradshaw in turn is suspicious, even aggressive towards 'cultivated people' (p. 107). This contradiction in Clarissa cannot be evaded: her stoical, almost existential anguish and her creative energy in organising the party, on the one hand; her role as snobbish and superficial hostess of high society, on the other. This was Woolf's worry too: 'the doubtful point is, I think, the character of Mrs Dalloway. It may be too stiff, too glittering and tinsely'.[6] But because of the 'heavy, ugly, commonplace' (p. 137) nature of the accuser, Woolf can make her heroine's defence more convincing than it could otherwise have been.

But though Clarissa and Miss Kilman are starkly opposed, the novel does none the less propose a mediation of their antagonistic qualities in Lady Bruton, whom Clarissa in a sense envies. Like Kilman, Lady Bruton is a physically powerful, emphatically phallic woman. She is 'a strong martial woman' with a 'ramrod bearing' who 'could have worn the helmet and shot the arrow', thus contrasting with the physical slightness of Clarissa (p. 198). But like Clarissa, Lady Bruton belongs to the upper echelons of society and, unlike Miss Kilman, she has little intellect: 'Debarred by her sex, and some truancy, too, of the logical faculty (she found it impossible to write a letter to the *Times*)' (p. 198). 'Derived from the eighteenth century', she belongs decisively to the past. As an aristocrat, it is appropriate that the positive values associated with the body should attach to her, since the aristocracy as a class is defined by its blood and breeding. These values have migrated downwards socially, attaching themselves to the lower classes represented by Kilman and becoming negative and dystopian in the process. It is Kilman's fusion of mind and body that makes her, politically, so dangerous in the novel, for she incarnates two of the most potent middle-class images of social subversion. On the one hand, she is a menacing utopianist who constructs cerebral schemes for the total renovation of society. Hence her enthusiasm for post-revolutionary Russia, which places her in the Jacobin tradition first denounced in the name of piecemeal, 'organic' reform by Edmund Burke. Sally and Clarissa were enthusiastic over William Morris in their teens – 'they meant to found a society to abolish private property' (p. 36) – and such youthful infatuations, the novel implies, display an innocent idealism. Kilman falls out of favour because she has poor enough taste still to be adhering to socialist principles in her forties. But she is not only abstract revolutionary, but also represents the middle-class fear of the lower orders as 'mob', as a pre-rational body clamouring for gratification, violently overturning social constraints. Hence the novel's stress on Kilman's voracity: her wolfing down of eclairs, her desire for the sensory pleasures she has been deprived of. But in uniting these two images of revolution, she is also rendered powerless. Mind and body tug in opposite directions, and the overall effect is to leave Kilman static and impotent in the middle. Thus Clarissa finally defeats her because the 'abducted' Elizabeth returns to the family.

> Love and religion! thought Clarissa, going back into the drawing-room, tingling all over . . . The cruellest things in the world, she thought, seeing them clumsy, hot, domineering, hypocritical, eavesdropping, jealous, infinitely cruel and unscrupulous, dressed in mackintosh coat, on the landing; love and religion. Had she ever tried to convert anyone herself? Did she not wish everybody merely to be themselves? And she watched out of the window the old lady opposite climbing upstairs . . . . There was something solemn in it – but love and religion would destroy that, whatever it was, the privacy of the soul. The odious Kilman would destroy it.
>
> (pp. 138–9)

In these terms Clarissa defends herself over caring more for her roses than the Armenians: 'Hunted out of existence, maimed, frozen, the victims of cruelty and injustice . . . no, she could feel nothing for the Albanians, or was it the Armenians? but she loved her roses (didn't that help the Armenians?)' (p. 132). She asserts this in contrast to Kilman who 'would do anything for the Russians', 'starve[s] herself for the Austrians', but 'in private inflicted positive torture, so insensitive was she, dressed in a green mackintosh coat' (p. 12). Though Clarissa's argument is little more than a caricature, her point is that callousness of feeling causes oppression, and that it is therefore useless to react to injustice with the very kind of insensitivity which brought it into being in the first place. She rejects politics as incompetent; most areas of life 'can't be dealt with, she felt positive, by Acts of Parliament' (p. 4). However, a world groaning under injustice can hardly wait for a total change of the political system brought about simply by loving roses. Mrs Dalloway is such a 'pure' revolutionary that she ends up being reactionary. Though she feels the need for wholesale social transformation, she suspects the practical means of change (political action) as themselves bearing the dominative values of the system they are attacking. To attempt to transform society is, for Clarissa, to be complicit with its worst values. Even socialism is no more than a disguise for the tyrannical spirit of 'conversion'. It 'walks penitentially disguised as brotherly love through factories and parliaments; offers help, but desires power' (p. 110). This view is a further consequence of the Romantic suspicion of abstract political thought, and its effect is to leave Clarissa in a state of total political quiescence.

But the novel does not ignore the contradiction in Clarissa's views about society. Returning from her expedition to the florist, she reflects:

> how moments like this are buds on the tree of life . . . but all the more, she thought, taking up the pad, one must repay in daily life to servants, yes, to dogs and canaries, above all to Richard her husband, who was the foundation of it . . . one must pay back from this secret deposit of exquisite moments.
>
> (pp. 31–2)

But her guilty exquisite moments are ironised by being shaken the very next instant by the news that Lady Bruton had asked Richard to lunch without her. Earlier in the novel Mrs Dempster had already been used to satirise Clarissa's arguments about 'roses'. For Mrs Dempster, life has been bitter, she has given to it 'roses; figure; her feet too': 'Roses, she thought sardonically. All trash, m' dear. For . . . life had been no mere matter of roses' (p. 29).

Septimus is another victim of patriarchy, its 'scapegoat' (p. 27). He had left home as a boy 'because of his mother; she lied' (p. 92), and educated himself in public libraries. His growth is a process of breaking away from the Mother and assimilation to the locus of the Father. He works within capitalism, for a firm of auctioneers, valuers and estate agents, and finally goes to war in which he 'developed manliness'. But in this final stage of his cultivation of 'masculinity' Septimus has broken down: 'in the War itself he had failed' (p. 105). His obsession that 'one must be scientific' represents the imperative towards rationality of the patriarchal civilisation. But he at last finds that 'he could reason; he could read . . . he could add up his bill', but he could not feel: 'his brain was perfect; it must be the fault of the world then – that he could not feel' (p. 96).

Like Clarissa and Kilman, Septimus cannot come to terms with the body. 'His body was macerated until only the nerve fibres were left. It was spread like a veil upon a rock' (p. 62). He invokes a Shakespearean loathing of 'the sordidity of the mouth and the belly', and rejects his wife's wish to have a son: 'the business of copulation was filth to him before the end' (p. 97). But the refusal to procreate is also a refusal of the symbolic order. Septimus refuses to take the final step into patriarchy by becoming a father himself. His sense of being alone and helpless – 'exposed on this bleak eminence, stretched out' (p. 159) – is analogous to the fear of the infant bereft of the mother. He wishes to retrieve the maternal, which the Name-of-the-

Father forbids. Its bitterly resented prohibition is represented in the novel by Holmes and Bradshaw: 'What right has Bradshaw to say 'must' to me?' (p. 161). With the breakdown of the symbolic and the return of the repressed, Septimus loses the capacity for communication. He talks to himself, hears voices which do not exist, hears birds speak in Greek. Communication as the exchange of signs is made possible only within the symbolic order, through the split in the subject which is established by the intervention of the phallus in the unity with the mother. In Septimus' madness, the division between signifier and signified is no longer clear. Words and things are confused, imagination and reality no longer distinguishable. 'And the leaves being connected by millions of fibres with his own body, there on the seat, fanned it up and down; when the branch stretched he, too, made that statement' (p. 24). 'He was not Septimus now' (p. 25): he can no longer sustain a stable self, and body, world, word fuse, intersect and traverse each other. Inner meaning seems about to emerge from the world at any moment. The word is no longer an empty sign but an absolute reality through which truth shines with no dividing bar between signifier and signified: 'The word 'time' split its husk; poured its riches over him . . . ' (p. 76). Septimus had always been interested in poetry and now, released from the constraints of the symbolic order, he emerges as a paradigm of the symbolist poet. For him, 'Nature signified by some laughing hint . . . her determination to show . . . always beautifully, and standing up close to breathe through her hollowed hands Shakespeare's words, her meaning' (p. 153). When he escapes the 'forcing' of souls by a human nature that he conceives as 'the repulsive brute, with the blood-red nostrils':

> to watch a leaf quivering in the rush of air was an exquisite joy. Up in the sky swallows swooping, swerving, flinging themselves in and out, round and round, yet always with perfect control as if elastics held them; and the flies rising and falling; and the sun spotting now this leaf, now that, in mockery, dazzling it with soft gold in pure good temper; and now and again some chime (it might be a motor horn) tinkling divinely on the grass stalks – all of this, calm and reasonable as it was, made out of ordinary things as it was, was the truth now; beauty was everywhere.
>
> (p. 76)

In this state Septimus enjoys colours, rhythms, sounds with extreme intensity as the thetic subject is dissolved into the semiotic *chora* it had formerly so severely repressed.

However, the society which the Name-of-the-Father upholds does not leave one alone. It drives a wedge between subject and the maternal body, signifier and signified. Clarissa understands Septimus' suicide as 'defiance. Death was an attempt to communicate, people feeling the impossibility of reaching the centre which, mystically, evades them; closeness drew apart; rapture faded; one was alone. There was an embrace in death' (p. 202). In psychoanalytic terms, the 'embrace' which Septimus aims at in death may be regarded as an embrace with the Mother. It is impossible to reach the 'centre', since the subject is split in its very constitution. It is this embrace which Clarissa seems to experience for a moment with women: *jouissance*[7] which 'gushed and poured with an extraordinary alleviation over the cracks and sores' when she saw 'an inner meaning almost expressed' (p. 35).

What is crucial is not how Clarissa deciphers Septimus' suicide, but *that* she deciphers it, that a relation is established between the two figures. If Septimus does indeed 'embrace' the Mother in death, it is because he now in a sense *has* a 'mother' who acknowledges him: 'She felt somehow very like him' (p. 204). The novel is deeply marked by the images of the absent son and the grieving mother, and in this respect is a development of the closing pages of *Jacob's Room*.[8] Early on Clarissa thinks of Mrs Foxcroft 'eating her heart out because that nice boy was killed and now the old Manor House must go to a cousin; or Lady Bexborough who opened a bazaar, they said, with the telegram in her hand, John, her favourite, killed' (p. 5). Clarissa's thoughts revert several times to Lady Bexborough, for news of her son's death intrudes as brutally into her bazaar as news of Septimus' does into Clarissa's party. The figures of bereaved mother and absent son also haunt Peter Walsh's dreams: 'an elderly woman who seems . . . to seek over the desert, a lost son; to search for a rider destroyed; to be the figure of the mother whose sons have been killed in the battles of the world' (p. 63). When Clarissa 'understands' Septimus' suicide she momentarily assumes the guise of this archetypal bereaved mother.

Though Septimus perished under the pressure of a patriarchal society, Clarissa 'had escaped' by submitting herself to the Law and obtaining protection:

> there was the terror; the overwhelming incapacity, one's parents giving it into one's hands, this life, to be lived to the end, to be walked with serenely; there was in the depths of her heart an awful fear. Even now,

quite often if Richard had not been there reading the *Times* . . . she
must have perished. She had escaped. But that young man had killed
himself.

(pp. 202–3)

She concedes her compromises, 'her disgrace . . . She had schemed;
she had pilfered . . . She had wanted success' (p. 203). In contrast, the
old woman in the house opposite affirms the imperishable existence
of the soul, which entirely escapes the social world. She represents a
woman's space, a room of one's own, independent of male-domi-
nated society. By means of this mirror image of her self – 'the old
lady stared straight at her!' (p. 203) – Clarissa can secure this female
space in herself.

Clarissa survives despite or perhaps because of her contradictions;
Septimus vicariously represents the risk of a total rejection of patriarchal law, and perishes. He is both the absent son, united with the
mother only in the Pyrrhic moment of death, and a surrogate for
Clarissa, committing suicide on her behalf. In Woolf's original plan
Clarissa was herself to die.[9] The invention of Septimus is thus a
defensive 'splitting', whereby Clarissa's most dangerous impulses are
projected into another figure who can die for her; to this extent, she
and he are one composite character. The internal split in Clarissa
which worried Woolf – existential anguish versus social superficiality
– reveals that the problem of woman opens on to the problems of
subjectivity and of writing. How is it possible to recognise and
valorise the position of woman as difference? There are two obvious
ways open to feminists. One may deny the difference in order to be
admitted as subject in the symbolic order, becoming a token man. Or
one may refuse the symbolic altogether, and risk being even more
marginalised than before or, worse, expelled as mad from society.
These alternatives are in a sense represented by Kilman and Septimus;
Clarissa must negotiate a precarious balance between them. Either
way, a woman is grievously at risk. Clarissa sees her sister Sylvia, 'on
the verge of life, the most gifted of them', killed by a falling tree – 'all
Justin Parry's fault' (p. 85). The Father kills the most gifted girl by
means of the Phallus (tree). No wonder then that Clarissa 'always
had the feeling that it was very, very dangerous to live even one day'
(p. 9). Hence her strategy of wariness: 'her notion being that the
Gods, who never lost a chance of hurting, thwarting and spoiling
human lives, were seriously put out if, all the same, you behaved like
a lady' (p. 85), and we can rewrite 'gods' here as 'men'. To behave

'like a lady', as patriarchy's 'perfect hostess', is thus a cautious programme for survival.

To avoid total submission to the Law of the Father, gaining a place in the symbolic at the price of negating women's difference, but also to avoid expulsion from the symbolic into complete silence: one can only oscillate between these two positions, living a tension which must not be fully resolved in either direction. A woman must reject the frozen identity of the subject but not relinquish subject-hood altogether.

From Makiko Minow-Pinkney, *Virginia Woolf and the Problem of the Subject: Feminine Writing in the Major Novels* (Brighton, 1987), pp. 70–81.

NOTES

[This essay is from Minow-Pinkney's chapter on *Mrs Dalloway* in her book on Virginia Woolf. The book is a prolonged exploration of the possibilities of reading Woolf in terms of the theories of Julia Kristeva. In the earlier part of the chapter, not printed here, Minow-Pinkney uses close linguistic analysis alongside Kristevan theory to describe the novel's narrative voice. She does not see it as J. Hillis Miller's coherent 'omniscient narrator' (see p. 45 above), but as something 'fractured, wavering, multiple' and as 'a denial of the unified subject which supports all discourse and is necessarily "masculine"', since the symbolic order is established with the phallus as its fundamental signifier' (*Virginia Woolf and the Problem of the Subject*, p. 58). She sees the narration of *Mrs Dalloway* as a continuous disruption of the very possibility of a unified rational account of events, which can only be produced by a voice that represses the chaotic pre-language union with the mother. She goes on, in the piece reprinted here, to demonstrate how the characters themselves enact the struggle, described by Kristeva, between the original love for the mother and the patriarchal repression of this in society and the rational order. In a brief final passage (*Virginia Woolf and the Problem of the Subject*, pp. 81–3) she goes on to describe the novel as a dialectic between 'stasis and rupture', 'dissemination and reconstruction', and as asking how women can voice their own consciousness, still close to the original bond with the mother, without being 'mad'. These are complex theories, but readers new to them will find a helpful account of some of Kristeva's work in Toril Moi's essay (p. 87 above). They will also find that Minow-Pinkney's discussion of *Mrs Dalloway* itself clarifies some of the theory just by relating it to the Woolf novel; and that the result is an illuminating account of current ideas about the body, the link with the mother, and society.

As throughout this volume, references to *Mrs Dalloway* are to the Penguin edition with an Introduction and Notes by Elaine Showalter and text edited by Stella McNichol (London, 1992). Ed.]

1. Julia Kristeva, *Polylogue* (Paris, 1977), p. 79, cited in Josette Feral, 'Antigone or the Irony of the Tribe', *Diacritics*, 10: 3 (September 1978), 12.

2. Susan Dick (ed.), *The Complete Shorter Fiction of Virginia Woolf* (London, 1985), p. 146.

3. [Kristeva uses the term *chora* to represent the place in which consciousness retains the non-symbolic drives of babyhood and union with the mother, seen in rhythm, laughter, even word-games where the words do not *mean*. It is in opposition to signification where meanings are apparently -made, as by words that represent something other than themselves. (See Kristeva, selections from 'Revolution in Poetic Language', in Toril Moi (ed.), *The Kristeva Reader* [Oxford, 1986], pp. 89–136.) Earlier in the chapter in *Virginia Woolf and the Problem of the Subject* (pp. 63–4), Minow-Pinkney has suggested that sea imagery which the narrative attaches to Clarissa (*Mrs Dalloway*, p. 43) and to Septimus (p. 153) indicates and at the same time controls the semiotic *chora*. Ed.]

4. I use this phrase ['phallic woman' Ed.] in its generalised, non-psychoanalytical sense. 'It should be pointed out that this expression is often employed in a loose way as a description of a woman with allegedly masculine character traits – e.g. authoritarianism – even when it is not known what the underlying phantasies are.' (J. Laplanche and J.-B. Pontalis, *The Language of Psycho-Analysis*, trans. Donald Nicholson-Smith [London, 1973], p. 312).

5. Raymond Williams, 'The Bloomsbury Fraction', *Problems of Materialism and Culture: Selected Essays* (London, 1980), p. 312.

6. Leonard Woolf (ed.), *A Writer's Diary. Being Extracts from the Diary of Virginia Woolf* (London, 1953), p. 61.

7. The French term *jouissance* carries a wide range of meaning: enjoyment in the sense of legal or social possession, pleasure, and the pleasure of sexual climax. Lacan uses the word emphasising the *totality* of enjoyment covered by it – simultaneously sexual, spiritual, physical, conceptual. Kristeva similarly uses the word to denote a total joy which 'also, through the working of the signifier . . . implies the presence of meaning (*jouissance* = *J'ouis sens* = I heard meaning), requiring it by going beyond' (Julia Kristeva, *Desire in Language: A Semiotic Approach to Literature and Art*, ed. Leon S. Roudiez [Oxford, 1980], p. 16). In Kristeva's work, purely sensual or sexual pleasure is covered by the term *plaisir*.

8. Virginia Woolf, *Jacob's Room* (London, 1922).

9. [Minow-Pinkney's note reads: 'See the preface to the first edition of *Mrs Dalloway*. In a letter Woolf wrote "Septimus and Mrs Dalloway should be entirely dependent upon each other" (Nigel Nicholson and Joanne Trautmann (eds), *The Letters of Virginia Woolf*, vol. 3 [London and New York, 1977], p. 189.' But see also my note 6 to David Lodge's essay, p. 32 above. Ed.]

8

'Cam the Wicked': Woolf's Portrait of the Artist as her Father's Daughter

ELIZABETH ABEL

> I'm now all on the strain with desire to stop journalism & get on to *To the Lighthouse*. . . . the centre is father's character, sitting in a boat, reciting We perished, each alone, while he crushes a dying mackerel – however, I must refrain.
>
> (Entry for 14 May 1925, *Diary*, vol. 3)[1]

> Then one day walking round Tavistock Square I made up, as I sometimes make up my books, *To the Lighthouse*; in a great, apparently involuntary rush. . . . I wrote the book very quickly; and when it was written, I ceased to be obsessed by my mother. I no longer hear her voice; I do not see her . . . .
>
> Certainly, there she was, in the very centre of that great Cathedral space which was childhood; there she was from the very first.
>
> ('A Sketch of the Past', 1939)[2]

If *Mrs Dalloway* is constructed such that 'every scene would build up the idea' of its central character, *To the Lighthouse* is in doubt about its centre.[3] Resisting a unitary focus, the text enacts the problematics of recounting a family history whose plural subject fosters diverse narratives. *To the Lighthouse* dramatises the contradictions between Woolf's prospective and retrospective definitions of its centre. The lacuna 'Time Passes' offers as a textual centre is only the most striking manifestation of a discontinuity sustained more discretely through the multiple histories Woolf hoped would counteract the

112

sentimentality threatened by her theme: 'The word 'sentimental' sticks in my gizzard. . . . But this theme may be sentimental; father and mother and child in the garden; the sail to the Lighthouse. I think, though, that when I begin it I shall enrich it in all sorts of ways; thicken it; give it branches – roots – which I do not perceive now'. [4] Woolf's metaphors of textual enrichment have changed since *Mrs Dalloway*: the 'beautiful caves' that were to deepen private history have been exchanged for metaphors of thickening drawn from the interdependent parts of a tree: a family tree that will ironise the family romance by matching its plural subject to a plural narrative. Chronology has also grown more complex, for the straightforward movement of history, which reverses Woolf's evolving vision of the text by progressing from mother to father, is countered by the multiple acts of retrospection that advance the narrative by moving back.

It is this heterogeneity, this insistence on representing its own narrative ambivalence, that has been neglected in the criticism, which has concentrated primarily on specific aspects of Woolf's 'theme', usually focusing either on the variations on androgyny played by the Ramsays (not only male/female, but also its permutations: fact/ imagination, reason/intuition, truth/beauty, [mock] heroism/domesticity, farsightedness/myopia, and so on) or on the dilemma of the woman artist dramatised by Lily Briscoe. Although analyses of genre have taken as their starting-point Woolf's own uncertainty about the appropriate label for her text, they have tended to translate her indecision into an assertion. Thus, the question mark disappears from her claim that 'I am making up *To the Lighthouse* – the sea is to be heard all through it. I have an idea that I will invent a new name for my books to supplant "novel". A new —— by Virginia Woolf. But what? Elegy?'[5] Circumscribing genre unifies a text whose origins and broadest patterns may be elegiac, but whose fractured explorations of elegiac subjects resists consolidation as a single genre or theme.

Like other critical perspectives on this text, a reading that focuses on self-reflexive narrative anticipates *A Room of One's Own*, where Woolf conflates the dynamics of the family romance with those of narrative by mapping family metaphors onto literary processes: 'we think back through our mothers if we are women'.[6] In *To the Lighthouse* the familial context, accentuated by the island setting, is also the arena of self-conscious narrative, though here the claims of patrilinearity compete with those of matrilinearity. It is this extended overlap, not the episodic and explicit Freudian allusions critics have decried, that makes this Woolf's most profoundly psychoanalytic text. *To the Lighthouse* is shot through with scenes of reading, writing and painting, inconspicuous yet germinal scenes from which memory spins its tale, textual moments (in Lily Briscoe's words) 'ringed round, lit up, visible to the last detail, with all before it blank and all after it blank, for miles and miles' (p. 186). This is a text concerned not only with the genesis of narrative, but with different models of textuality and their relation to their narrator's and subject's sexuality. These links among family history, narrative and gender constitute the psychoanalytic substance of this text, which refracts its author's narrative concerns among its disparate characters. Thus, Woolf's two most explicit textual representatives – Lily and Cam – inherit her competing narrative loyalties. Lily is her vehicle for thinking back through her mother. Heir to her author's original plan of centring her text on 'father's character, sitting in a boat, reciting We perished, each alone', Cam enables Woolf to dramatise the narrative plight of the daughter who thinks back through her father.

Because critics have systematically neglected Cam in favour of Lily and James, who are accented and counterpointed in the text, this essay plucks her from the web of narrative to illuminate, and account for, her obscurity. By her name and her position as the youngest Ramsay daughter, Cam is Woolf's most literal narrative counterpart, her self-portrait as her father's daughter, yet she is powerfully, though erratically, submerged. Minimally outlined in Part I, Cam nevertheless joins the finale in Part III – and yet, as such a shadowy, attenuated presence that it is not clear why she is included. The arrival at the Lighthouse caps James's drama exclusively: Cam has never desired this journey and drifts suspended between the text's dual resolutions: the arrival at the Lighthouse and the completion of Lily's painting. Yet, rather than a sign of aesthetic incoherence, her plight brilliantly discloses one intersection of psychoanalysis and narrative: the imaginative field delimited by the daughter's shift from pre-Oedipal mother to Oedipal father. In this later, more self-conscious work, Woolf has rewritten Clarissa Dalloway's story to accent an eroticised relation with the body of the father's texts. Paternal violence has softened to a seduction that is more textual than sexual, but that cuts the daughter as decisively from her maternal past. Purposefully obscure, Cam anticipates the problematic Woolf who announces two years later in *A Room of One's Own*: 'It is useless to go to the great male writers for help, however much one may go to them for pleasure. . . . The ape is too distant to be sedulous' (p. 76).

Cam is an enigma throughout the text. Less central than James, she is also less psychoanalytically programmatic: no ritualistic images (such as the axes, knives and pokers with which James fantasises murdering his father) allegorise her consciousness. As a child, she is fiercely independent: 'She would not 'give a flower to the gentleman' as the nursemaid told her. No! no! no! she would not' (*To the Lighthouse*, p. 26). Hence her appellation by Mr Bankes: 'Cam the Wicked' (p. 27). Indecipherable even to her mother (and perhaps the only character who is), Cam seems wholly present to herself as she dashes through Part I like a projectile guided by some urgent private desire: 'She was off like a bird, bullet, or arrow, impelled by what desire, shot by whom, at what directed, who could say? What, what? Mrs Ramsay pondered, watching her' (p. 61). This defiant energy has dissipated by Part III; Cam sits passively in the boat while her brother navigates, her father reads and chats with Macalister, and Macalister's boy catches fish. Like the boat that bobs up and down in place, Cam's thoughts circle back on themselves as she aimlessly dabbles her hand in the water and watches the fish that objectify her feeling of entrapment. Whereas the narrative holds James psychically responsible for the interrupted progress of the boat by linking his drama of memory and repression to the rise and fall of the wind (section 8), thereby according him the task of reshaping the past to enable the future, Cam's internal drama (section 10), which follows and depends on her brother's, is severed from this narrative teleology. James faces the Lighthouse and navigates toward it; Cam sits in the bow and gazes back toward the island. Though brother and sister share the task of reconstructing memory, Cam's efforts do not impinge on the action. Her project is purely historical.

At the beginning of 'The Lighthouse', the cowed and angry siblings share a single will, though Cam's syntactic subordination – 'He would be impatient in a moment, James thought, and Cam thought' (p. 177). 'So James could tell, so Cam could tell' (p. 179) – indicates the hierarchy. Woolf chooses the occasion of an interpolated story to introduce Cam as an independent consciousness. Macalister's tale of maritime rescue and disaster, prompted by Mr Ramsay's questions about the great storm at Christmas, weaves an alliance between the two old men, overcoming class and ethnic difference to constitute a homogeneous narrative voice as Mr Ramsay adjusts his gaze and speech to Macalister's and mimics his Scottish accent. Shared pleasure in the sexual division of labour and its representation in narrative outweighs other differences: Mr Ramsay 'liked that men should labour and sweat on the windy beach at night . . . he liked men to work like that, and women to keep house and sit beside sleeping children indoors, while men were drowned, out there in a storm' (p. 179). Woolf dramatises the impact of this story not on James, who can aspire to a future role in it, but on its more problematic female auditor, whose access to this explicitly masculine discourse requires mediation. The imaginative arena the story opens frees the carefully guarded love Cam feels for her father, but this release is qualified by the mental act it presupposes. Cam can enter this discourse only by-displacing herself as its potential subject, transferring her childhood love of adventure to an idealised image of her (elderly) father, with some consequent mystification of her own emotions. 'Cam thought, feeling proud of him *without knowing quite why*, had he been there he would have launched the lifeboat, he would have reached the wreck. . . . He was so brave, he was so adventurous' (p. 179: emphasis added). Woolf marks Cam's emergence in the third part of her text as a reaction to a masculine 'text' that grants her the gendered relationship to narrative explored in *A Room of One's Own*.

Cam's idealisation of Mr Ramsay, moreover, provokes a return of what it has repressed: the knowledge of his tyranny. This knowledge is Cam's as well as James's, and the 'compact' that declares it and that suddenly checks her surge of affection for her father has presumably been forged by both siblings, who had 'vowed, in silence, as they walked, to stand by each other and carry out the great compact – to resist tyranny to the death' (*To the Lighthouse*, p. 178). Yet Cam perceives the agreement as a text she can neither revise, revoke, nor fully endorse, a coercive force that evolves into 'the tablets of eternal wisdom' lying on the knee of James the lawgiver, silencing her (p. 183). Cam is complicit in this silencing. Though the compact *does* represent James's perspective more fully than her own, and *does* reflect his greater authority, Cam's desire to evade her own anger obscures her part in the creation of an unwritten text that records a strand of her relation to her father. As she projects her former adventurousness onto her father, she projects onto her brother her former defiance, the voice that had said 'No! no! no!' to the gentleman, dividing her salient childhood traits between two men and two texts in which participation leads to alienation. Denying herself the roles of both protagonist and author, she colludes with the assumptions of patriarchal textuality. The scene on the boat suggests some prior learning.

Paralysed by the stand-off between her father and her brother, Cam recovers her own memories only after this drama is resolved in section 8 and the boat is speeding toward the Lighthouse once again. In section 10 the motion sparks Cam's imagination, which converts the growing distance into time and reverts to a single privileged scene, her counterpart to James's epiphanic vision of his mother 'saying simply whatever came into her head. She alone spoke the truth; to her alone could he speak it' (p. 203). Cam, however, remembers her father, not her mother; scenes of reading and writing rather than of speech; and a study rather than a garden. Eden to her is the garden's aftermath, though the narrative suggests this revision is delusion. Her memory focuses on her father's study. 'Sometimes she strayed in from the garden purposely to catch them at it. There they were (it might be Mr Carmichael or Mr Bankes who was sitting with her father) sitting opposite each other in their low armchairs. . . . Just to please herself she would take a book from the shelf and stand there, watching her father write' (p. 205). In Cam's imagination, fathers know best, and they speak the knowledge of the printed text. 'They were crackling in front of them the pages of *The Times*, when she came in from the garden, all in a muddle about something some one had said about Christ, or hearing that a mammoth had been dug up in a London street, or wondering what Napoleon was like' (p. 205). 'Straying' from garden to study, from nature to culture, from the private muddle to the public text, Cam re-enacts Clarissa Dalloway's symbolic moment of transition from pastoral Bourton to urban London, and from Sally Seton to Richard Dalloway, the moment sealed during Clarissa's retreat from her party to the private room in which she assimilates Septimus Smith's death by renouncing the hold of her past. Explicitly, the two scenes are linked through the reference to *The Times*, which reassures the female spectator that the flux of experience can be securely captured in the authoritative idiom of the daily patriarchal text. Clarissa's speculation that 'Even now, quite often if Richard had not been there reading the *Times*, so that she could crouch like a bird and gradually revive . . . she must have perished' prepares for the startling reversal: 'And once she had walked on the terrace at Bourton. It was due to Richard; she had never been so happy' (*Mrs Dalloway*, p. 203). More profoundly, the scenes are linked by the desire to mark the closure of a developmental era.

In Cam's memory, closure is gentle, a gradual transition from one sphere to another, a gradual translation of experience to thought that unfolds organically like a leaf that has gained, not lost, its natural environment. As a child in the study Cam had felt that 'one could let whatever one thought expand here like a leaf in water; and if it did well here, among the old gentlemen smoking and *The Times* crackling then it was right' (*To the Lighthouse*, p. 205). Yet the tension between her metaphor and her literal description undercuts her evolutionary model, reasserting a distinction she would blur. Throughout the text Cam associates the leaf with Mrs Ramsay. In 'The Window' Cam carries a leaf when she responds to her mother's call; in 'The Lighthouse' the leaf is her recurrent image for the island that incarnates the receding past. 'It lay like that on the sea, did it, with a dent in the middle and two sharp crags, and the sea swept in there, and spread away for miles and miles on either side of the island. It was very small; shaped something like a leaf stood on end' (p. 204). Cam's simile revises but does not conceal a prior, less overt metaphorisation of the island as a female body, a womb, from which she is drawn slowly away. With a sea-swept dent in the middle of two crags, the island hovering behind the leaf is a figure of the mother. As a child, Cam hoped to extend, articulate and assess the past identified with the garden and the mother by translating the leaf into the language of the father – and in so doing to imitate her father's own translations of hedges into periods, of geranium leaves into 'scraps of paper on which one scribbles notes in the rush of reading' (p. 48), of nature's leaves into the pages of a book. When she repeats this gesture in the present, a fissure surfaces. It is the image of the leaf-shaped island that triggers her adolescent memory: 'Small as it was, and shaped something like a leaf stood on its end with the gold-sprinkled waters flowing in and about it, it had, she supposed, a place in the universe – even that little island? The old gentlemen in the study she thought could have told her. Sometimes she strayed in from the garden . . . ' (p. 205). The rift between the gold-sprinkled island and the old men in the study reveals what has been lost in the translation and what now is lost more emphatically in Cam's attempt to situate one domain of experience within the discourse of another.

Only these repercussions of the past in the present lend credibility to the hints of a Fall. If the young Cam 'strays' from the garden in search of information, this knowledge is not forbidden, nor is she expelled. The garden, moreover, is no unfallen natural paradise, for voices within it have produced the muddle that sends her in search of clarification. If there is a Fall, it pertains not to the search for knowledge, or even to its source (the study is a logical, perhaps inevitable, resource to enlist), but to its consequences. The historical questions that arise in the garden – about Christ, Napoleon and a prehistoric mammoth – are appropriately carried to the study, but they differ from the issue the older Cam mentally refers to the same place: a question of personal history, of the private past, of the mother's place 'in the universe'. However passionately motivated her search for knowledge, and however legitimate her indebtedness to her father, Cam is apprenticeship in the study ensnares as well as liberates her, sanctioning certain modes of thought, discouraging others, creating an intellectual framework that becomes her single frame of reference. The old gentlemen in the study reinforce Cam's interest in history, priming her for the position she assumes in the boat. Studying the past, she also learns to privilege it. By 'The Lighthouse' Cam's expert at gazing backward, at translating images of a shifting present into the framework of the past, at repeating in adolescence patterns learned as a child.

The scene in the study both mirrors and prepares the scene in the boat. Cam's psychological position in the present, as well as her literal one, moreover, finds a precedent in her father's study. In both situations Cam's curiosity and responsiveness draw her imaginatively into a conversation between men, with a consequent erosion of her own subjectivity. As the two scenes blur in her mind, similarities emerge between her relation to the story spun by Mr Ramsay and Macalister, and her relation to the dialogue between Mr Ramsay and an old gentleman 'who might be Mr Carmichael or Mr Bankes', whose identity matters less than his structural position opposite her father, Macalister's position. (We are told this location obliquely through stage directions: when James fears his father's admonition about a slackening sail, he imagines that Mr Ramsay 'would say sharply, "Look out! Look out!" and old Macalister would turn slowly on his seat – presumably to look at the drooping sail; when Mr Ramsay listens to Macalister's story, he leans forward – presumably to catch every word [p. 179].) In the study, ambiguity obscures who talks with whom. Cam wants to believe that her questions received answers, but the text suggests that the gentlemen conversed primarily with one another. Whom did they address when they turned their papers, crossed their knees, 'and said something now and then very brief' (p. 205)? An almost identical phrase in the next sentence records a conversation between the two old men: Mr Ramsay said something 'briefly to the other old gentleman opposite' (p. 205). Only in Cam's final recapitulation of the scene does someone explicitly answer her question: 'The old gentleman, lowering the paper suddenly, said something very brief over the top of it about the character of Napoleon' (p. 207). Is this a wishful secondary revision, part of her project of rescuing her father from James's hostile fantasy? The substance of the interaction reinforces its structural ambiguity. Cam's only question to be answered, and the only specified content of any verbal exchange, concerns the character of Napoleon, ominous in light of Woolf's subsequent depiction of this historical figure. In *A Room of One's Own* Woolf explains that 'mirrors are essential to all violent and heroic action. That is why Napoleon and Mussolini both insist so emphatically upon the inferiority of women, for if they were not inferior, they would cease to enlarge'.[7] By *The Years*, 'the character of Napoleon' has evolved into 'the psychology of great men', exemplified explicitly by Napoleon, that obstructs the knowledge of 'ourselves, ordinary people' (women, homosexuals, foreigners, in this context), which would enable us to make 'laws and religions that fit' – in contrast, presumably, to such homogenising codes as the 'tablets of eternal wisdom' transmitted from father to son.[8] For Woolf, Napoleon incarnates the attitude that writes women out of a history defined as exchanges between (great) men. That his character should be the climax of a scene in which Cam struggles to learn history reveals the pathos of her eagerness for access to a discourse whose terms diminish her, and for a place in an exchange that calls into question her status as interlocutor.

The apprenticeship in the study is not the only source of Cam's attenuation in language. It may be her fate as youngest daughter to serve as a vehicle of messages rather than their sender or recipient, and her willing metamorphosis into a blank page encourages her use as a transparent medium. The significant variable is the gender of the speakers. In 'The Window' Woolf briefly sketches an alternative semiotic context for Cam. When sent by Mrs Ramsay to ask the cook if Andrew, Paul, and Minta have returned from the beach, Cam mimics for her mother the cook's exact response. But between the question and the answer she inserts her own story, and 'it was only by waiting patiently, and hearing that there was an old woman in the kitchen with very red cheeks, drinking soup out of a basin, that Mrs Ramsay at last prompted that parrot-like instinct which had picked up Mildred's words quite accurately and could now produce them, if one waited, in a colourless singsong' (*To the Lighthouse*, p. 61). A diminutive female Hermes shuttling between two female speakers, Cam nevertheless succeeds in imposing her own embryonic narrative. Its subject, 'an old woman in the kitchen', resonates against Woolf's first description of the centre of her text, the vision to which Cam is heir: the father in a boat. The text associates the red-cheeked old woman with the bibulous elderly cleaning-woman Mrs McNab, who in 'Time Passes' remembers being 'always welcome in the kitchen' where the cook, at Mrs Ramsay's request, kept a plate of milk soup for her. Though stripped of Mrs Ramsay's arabesquing consciousness, Mrs McNab serves in 'Time Passes' as a bare corporeal remainder and reminder of her mistress, an incarnation of memory who tears the 'veil of silence' that has fallen on the Ramsay home (p. 142). As the lowest common denominator of female artistry, the work of preservation whose psychological correlate Mrs Ramsay calls 'the effort of merging and flowing and creating' (p. 91), Mrs McNab is the figure who by sheer determination rescues the Ramsay's home from 'the sands of oblivion' and connects the first part of the novel to the third (p. 151). As Cam's kitchen muse, she fleetingly inspires a story that refuses to be squelched. In the same way that her position in the novel inscribes the traces of female labour in a bleakly inhuman textual centre, her position in Cam's circuit as messenger raises the prospect of a third rendition of the novel's three-part form. Cam's vision of the island as a sea-swept dent between two crags hints at this rendition. The configuration of mass and space shows a family resemblance with Lily Briscoe's 'question . . . how to connect this mass on the right hand with that on the left' (p. 60) and James's 'night's darkness' between two days (p. 7), but Cam represents the centre as a place of origin. Her glimpse of the island shares with her miniature narrative a buried notion of female engendering. These echoing accounts could evolve into Cam's counterpart to the narrative formulas offered by Lily and James; they could become Cam's story, her meta-narrative, her version of history. But this nascent narrative design never emerges, and cannot emerge. Cam's muted presence in the text is no accident, for it is precisely when she first perceives the island as a body – 'She had never seen it from out at sea before' (p. 204) – that she turns to the memory of the study.

Cam's poignancy derives from a narrative perspective that blends sympathy with irony. It is less that we see options to which Cam is blind (to whom should she refer her questions about history?) than that we can gauge the cost of choices she has made, interpret metaphors opaque to her, and register her pleasure as an index of her innocence. Though Cam's course may look easier than James's, since the death of their mother appears less devastating to her and her father is less peremptory with her, we can also observe that, if her suffering is less acute and articulate, it is also less empowering. If James renounces a privileged bond with his mother and the unsullied truth her language signifies to him, and accepts in their place the poverty and power of linguistic signs (the tablets he inherits from his father), Cam never fully accedes to this symbolic register. Her own metaphors betray that her father's study, in which she takes such pleasure, offers her the material of language more readily than its significance. Within this sanctuary, Cam relishes tangible signs with no expectation that their content is available. She represents the old gentlemen's clarification of her muddle as a tactile, rather than a verbal, intervention: 'Then they took all this [muddle] with their clean hands (they wore grey-coloured clothes; they smelt of heather) and they brushed the scraps together . . . ' (p. 205). Instead of reading the book she takes from the shelf 'just to please herself', she watches her father write and admires the evenness of his lines without attempting to decipher their meaning. The scene on the boat mirrors this relation to paternal texts. Cam is both thoroughly familiar with, and ignorant of, the book in which her father is engrossed, 'the little book whose yellowish pages she knew, without knowing what was written on them. It was small; it was closely printed. . . . But what might be written in the book which had rounded its edges off in his pocket, she did not know. What he thought they none of them knew' (p. 206). The father as text, like the father's texts, remains hermetic to her, and her attempt to generalise this condition cracks against James's conviction that he and his father 'alone knew each other' (p. 200). Cam's image of the tiller's transformation into tablets marks her only conscious recognition of their father's differing legacies. These differences crystallise in the children's final interactions with Mr Ramsay. Cam's relationship with her father culminates in a silent gesture of paternal courtship, as Mr Ramsay hands her 'a ginger-bread nut, as if he were a great Spanish gentleman, she thought, handing a flower to a lady at a window (so courteous his manner was)' (p. 222). The father–son relationship concludes with the breaking of silence in the long-withheld 'Well done!' that answers James's unspoken desire for paternal recognition and praise (p. 223). Despite (or because of) Cam's delight in her father's courtly gesture, this resolution of their relationship implies that her apprenticeship did not fulfil its promise. Revising a Keatsian model of treacherous seduction as the failure of a (feminine) imagination to sustain its offer of transcendence, Woolf's father–daughter narrative outlines a seduction by a (masculine) tradition that reneges on its equation of knowledge and authority.

The 'most touching' of the 'life-giving affinities' between Leslie Stephen and his youngest daughter, according to Leon Edel, was Sir Leslie's gift on Virginia's twenty-first birthday of a ring and a declaration: she was, he averred, 'a very good daughter'. Oblivious to the dissonance of his metaphors, Edel explains. 'It was as if there were a marriage and also a laying on of hands, a literary succession. The father . . . performed a marriage between Virginia and the world of letters.'[9] Woolf herself, however, was well aware that being wed to a tradition was not being its heir, and she dramatised this difference in the Ramsay children's destinies. The personal inclinations of daughter, and of father, have little relevance to the course of events; Cam's education in the study prepares her to inherit her mother's position rather than her father's. Whether overtly enacted as dialogue, or mediating more subtly between a masculine authorship and readership, the textual tradition transmitted by the study returns its female initiate to the original female position between two gentlemen: between Ramsay and Macalister, between Ramsay and the generic old gentlemen, between Ramsay and his son – the nuclear masculine pair. The daughter's position thus slides imperceptibly into the mother's. Though the father–mother–son triad that prevailed in 'The Window' gives way in 'The Lighthouse' to a father–daughter–son triad, the median feminine position is unchanged. As the scene on the boat gradually re-creates its predecessor at the window (*To the Lighthouse*, Part I, section 7), the characters psychically alter their positions. Having explicitly established that Mr Ramsay sits 'in the middle of the boat between them (James steered; Cam sat alone in the bow)' (p. 177), Woolf inconsistently rearranges the protagonists to conform with the emotional topography. Cam's 'brother was most god-like, her father most suppliant. And to which did she yield, she thought, sitting between them, gazing at the shore . . . ' (p. 183). As Cam inherits her mother's middle position, for which her training in the study paradoxically has groomed her, Woolf dissects the configuration that silences the daughter.

Ostensibly, Mr Ramsay tries during the boat trip to engage his daughter in conversation, but Woolf portrays the scene as an unvoiced dialogue between Mr Ramsay and his son. After Mr Ramsay's opening question, we shift directly to James's response: 'Who was looking after the puppy today? he [Mr Ramsay] asked. Yes, thought James pitilessly, seeing his sister's head against the sail, now she'll give way. I shall be left to fight the tyrant alone' (p. 183). Mr Ramsay's second question similarly returns us to James's consciousness. Sliding pronouns ('she', 'her', 'they', 'somebody') replace Cam with Mrs Ramsay as the pressure of the struggle recalls its prototype, Mr Ramsay's interruption of James's idyll with his mother.

> She'll give way, James thought, as he watched a look come upon her face, a look he remembered. They look down, he thought, at their knitting or something. Then suddenly they look up. There was a flash of blue, he remembered, and then somebody sitting with him laughed, surrendered, and he was very angry. It must have been his mother, he thought, sitting on a low chair, with his father standing over her . . . a man had marched up and down and stopped dead, upright, over them.
>
> (pp. 183–4)

Having blurred his sister with his mother, James succeeds in adolescence where he failed as a child and prevents his father's victory. Torn between the irreconcilable demands of her father and his son, Cam succumbs to silence, unable to find a language for her own split desire.

In the present scene, Mr Ramsay is humble, not apparently engaged in any struggle, eager only to converse with his daughter. His motivation, however, mirrors his son's: like James, he uses Cam to replay and repair the past, though he tries to compensate to his wife through his daughter rather than exacting compensation from her. When Cam's uncertainty about the points of the compass recalls Mrs Ramsay's imprecision about the weather, Mr Ramsay merges daughter and mother: 'He thought, women are always like that; the vagueness of their minds is hopeless. . . . It had been so with her – his wife' (p. 182). Grieving for his wife, and feeling remorse over his anger at her, Mr Ramsay craves the solace of his daughter's approval. The scene on the boat thus becomes a scene of seduction that locates Cam between two men struggling to redo their relation to her mother: 'I will make her smile at me, Mr Ramsay thought' (p. 182). His manner is courteous, but his project is coercive. Though he struggles to suppress his longing for confirmation, Cam reads it clearly. 'And what was she going to call him [the puppy]? her father persisted. He had had a dog when he was a little boy, called Frisk . . . she wished, passionately, to move some obstacle that lay upon her tongue and say, Oh, yes, Frisk. I'll call him Frisk' (p. 184). In this competition for her tongue, Cam can be silenced by Mosaic tablets or echo a paternal language that suggests an Adamic ritual of naming: 'So she said nothing, but looked doggedly and sadly at the shore. . . . They have no suffering there, she thought' (p. 185).

Ironically, Cam's education in the tradition that situates her in a silent centre enables her to gloss the ramifications of this situation. Assuming her mother's place between Mr Ramsay's 'entreaty – forgive me, care for me' and James's exhortation, 'Resist him. Fight him' (p. 183), Cam feels herself divided not only between father and son, but also between the claims of pity and those of justice, the binary opposition that conventionally distinguishes the Christian from the Judaic tradition. The terms are transposed (the son advocates justice, the father pity), but their reversibility does not alter the female position as a pivot between two dispensations, a place where centrality amounts to mediation. Cam's allusive language also echoes classical tragedy, especially the Sophoclean trilogy that has been a reservoir of cultural paradigms. The 'god-like' brother and the 'suppliant' father between whom Cam imagines herself seated suggest incarnations of the same individual: Oedipus the King, regal lawmaker, god-like in his splendour, who becomes the blind old man, the homeless suppliant of *Oedipus at Colonus*, an aged hero guided by his daughter. Woman again is pivot of this transformation. Mother and daughter to both father and son, Cam also assumes these overlapping roles within the implied Oedipal drama. As stand-in for her mother, she holds the place of Jocasta to both Mr Ramsay and to James, who betters his father in the conflict over her. As daughter, she must also be Antigone (both daughter and half-sister to Jocasta), and forgive, nurture, and protect her father in his frail old age. As sister, however, she must be Antigone to James and select her role from the last play of the trilogy, where sororal loyalty to brother over 'father' (both her father's brother and her prospective father-in-law) is the principled, heroic choice of living death over ethical compromise. Cam wants to play both Antigone's roles, to be the loyal sister and the loving daughter, but James forbids her to play Antigone to her father, and Mr Ramsay tries to dissuade her from the bond with her brother. Paralysed between father and son, between two manifestations of a patriarchal God and two incarnations of Oedipus, Cam is the ambiguous mother and maid whose body is a fulcrum in the sequences of history and a page on which the tests and texts of masculinity are inscribed. The only escape is out of the body, the desire motivating the suicidal fantasy (another echo of Jocasta and Antigone) latent in Cam's envious gaze at the island, where people, it seems, 'had fallen asleep . . . were free like smoke, were free to come and go like ghosts' (p. 185).

Cam is released from these fantasies only after James resolves the conflict with his father that places her between the two men. Section 10 opens with a sense of liberation: to describe it, Cam tentatively adopts, and then rejects, a narrative model drawn from Macalister, a story about escaping from a sinking ship. Her search for images more appropriate to her own sense of adventure begins by echoing the language of her mother in Mrs Ramsay's only solitary scene, the moment of visionary eroticism elicited by the Lighthouse beam ('The Window', section 11):

> What then came next? Where were they going? From her hand, ice cold, held deep in the sea, there spurted up a fountain of joy at the change, at the escape, at the adventure (that she should be alive, that she should be there). And the drops falling from this sudden and unthinking foundation of joy fell here and there on the dark, the slumbrous shapes in her mind; shapes of a world not realised but turning in their darkness, catching here and there, a spark of light; Greece, Rome, Constantinople.
>
> (pp. 204–5)

Gazing at the past illumined by this anticipation of the future, at the leaf-shaped island transformed by 'gold-sprinkled waters', Cam identifies her distinctive narrative task: to hinge the maternal shape of the past with the fleetingly illumined shapes of the future by articulating the central place she occupies, turning her historical aptitude to an unwritten history. It is here that she remembers her father. The section ends with the disappearance of the island: 'the leaf was losing its sharpness. . . . The sea was more important now than the shore' (p. 207). The final words return to Macalister's story and to Mr Ramsay's refrain, as Cam 'murmured, dreamily, half-asleep, how we perished, each alone' (p. 207).

* * *

[In the original essay, there follows here a passage arguing that Minta's actions in the novel 'gloss' Cam's silence, her inability to voice her own narrative in opposition to that of the masculine world. Minta's story is indicated in the novel, but only through a series of gaps and oblique images. Ed.]

'If we continue to speak the same language to each other, we will reproduce the same story . . . ', Luce Irigaray insists. 'If we continue to speak this sameness, if we speak to each other as men have spoken for centuries, as they taught us to speak, we will fail each other. Again . . . Words will pass through our bodies, above our heads, disappear, make us disappear'.[10] A certain circularity marks Cam's narrative activity, for the story she tells is the story of how she came to tell that story. It is a paradigmatic story of the daughter who thinks back through her father, a story of narrative imprisonment. Woolf's feat in this text is to read the Oedipal narrative as an account of the daughter's shift to her father's dialogue with his son(s), a discourse that situates her (like her mother) in a median position between two men. The Oedipal narrative now accounts for an attenuated female language as well as sexuality, for a language that itself attenuates women's sexuality.

As Woolf's conception of the centre of her text shifted from father to mother, her narrative attention gravitated to the figure of Lily Briscoe, a peripheral character in the holograph manuscript. Mr Ramsay in a boat reciting, 'We perished, each alone', became a focus of the third part of a text whose longest, richest, opening portion is dominated by his wife, psychically and aesthetically resurrected in Part III by her surrogate daughter Lily, rather than by Cam. Though Cam is overshadowed by this more successfully articulate 'sister', she nevertheless performs a vital function in disclosing the narrative costs of paternal filiation. Through Cam as well as Lily, then, Woolf adumbrates the claim from which much of her current pre-eminence in feminist literary history derives: 'we think back through our mothers if we are women'.[11]

From Jane Marcus (ed.), *Virginia Woolf and Bloomsbury. A Centenary Celebration* (London and Indiana, 1987), pp. 170–88.

NOTES

[Elizabeth Abel reads Woolf as articulating a theory of femininity closely parallel to the account which Freud was evolving during the same years. In this theory children break their infantile identity, and desire to possess their mother, at the oedipal crisis: male children move to take up the positive masculine identity identified with their father, and female children adopt the passive identity associated with their mother. Abel reads the stories of James and Cam as dramatisations of these events.

When this essay first appeared it was accompanied by a detailed commentary in footnotes which for reasons of space cannot be included here. In much of this commentary Abel reinforces the essay's account of *To the Lighthouse* as a version of Freudian theory concerned with the idea of silenced feminine identity. She also draws attention to a number of critics who refer, sometimes with distaste, to the parallel between James's story and Freud's oedipal narrative of a masculine subject (see my note to Mepham's essay, p. 44 above). In addition, she suggests autobiographical links between Cam and Virginia Woolf.

Abel has also written an essay on *Mrs Dalloway*, 'Narrative Structure(s) and Female Development: The Case of *Mrs Dalloway*' (in Elizabeth Abel et al. [eds], *The Voyage In: Fictions of Female Development* [Hanover and London, 1983]). This essay, which is discussed by Rachel Bowlby (pp. 147–8 below), reads Clarissa Dalloway's story as an account of female development which was subsequently paralleled in Freud's work: as an image of the trauma endured by females who have, in Abel's account of Freudian theory, to transfer from mother-love and pre-oedipal feminine bonding to female heterosexuality, and an image of the sexual repression involved. In revised forms both these essays became part of Abel's book *Virginia Woolf and the Fictions of Psychoanalysis* (Chicago, 1989).

As throughout this volume, references to *Mrs Dalloway* are to the Penguin edition with an Introduction and Notes by Elaine Showalter and text edited by Stella McNichol (London, 1992); and references to *To the Lighthouse* are to the Penguin edition with Introduction and Notes by Hermione Lee and text edited by Stella McNichol (London, 1992) Ed.]

1. *The Diary of Virginia Woolf*, vol. 3: *1925–30*, ed. Anne Olivier Bell with Andrew McNeillie (London and New York, 1980; Penguin edition, 1982), pp. 18–19.

2. Virginia Woolf, *Moments of Being: Unpublished Autobiographical Writings*, ed. Jeanne Schulkind (London and New York, 1976; Triad Panther edition, 1978), p. 94.

3. [Abel's original note here cites: 'Virginia Woolf, 18 June 1923, entry in holograph notebook dated variously from 9 November 1922 to 2 August 1923; cited in Charles G. Hoffmann, "From Short Story to Novel: The Manuscript Revisions of Virginia Woolf's *Mrs Dalloway*", *Modern Fiction Studies*, 14: 2 (Summer 1968), 183.' Ed.]

4. *The Diary of Virginia Woolf*, vol. 3: *1925–30*, p. 36: entry for 20 July 1925.

5. Ibid., p. 34: entry for 27 June 1925.

6. Virginia Woolf, *A Room of One's Own* (London, 1928; Penguin edition, 1945, 1992), p. 76. All further references are to this edition.

7. *A Room of One's Own*, p. 37.

8. Virginia Woolf, *The Years* (London and New York, 1937; New York edition), pp. 281–2.

9. Leon Edel, *Bloomsbury: A House of Lions* (London and New York, 1979; Harmondsworth, 1981), p. 92.

10. Luce Irigaray, 'When Our Lips Speak together', trans. Carolyn Burke from *Ce Sexe qui n'en est pas un* (Paris, 1977), in *Signs*, 6:1 (Autumn 1980), 69.

11. *A Room of One's Own*, p. 76.

9

Mothers and Daughters in Virginia Woolf's Victorian Novel

MARGARET HOMANS

In *A Room of One's Own*, celebrating the value of a women's literary tradition and of her own heritage of strong ancestresses, Woolf exhorts women writers to 'think back through our mothers'.[1] And yet as Jane Marcus points out, the women in Woolf's family were 'collaborators in their own oppression'.[2] Woolf's literary ancestresses, too, offered her at best an ambiguous heritage, whose drawbacks she if anything exaggerates. In *A Room of One's Own*, Woolf's account of literary women in history does as much to take away their accomplishments as it does to celebrate their courage. In 'Professions for Women' she writes of how, in order to write, she herself had to kill the 'Angel in the House', that Victorian matron who 'excelled in the difficult arts of family life', 'sacrificed herself daily', and insisted that women 'must charm, they must conciliate, they must – to put it bluntly – tell lies if they are to succeed.'[3] . . . The Angel in *To the Lighthouse* . . . is Mrs Ramsay, but Mrs Ramsay also embodies the enormous positive value Woolf finds in 'think[ing] back through our mothers'. Mrs Ramsay is Woolf's summary of nineteenth-century ideologies of motherhood, and the novel embodies Woolf's ambivalence about Victorian mothers. At the same time, as the daughter of a Victorian mother and of a Victorian tradition of literary women, Woolf uses the novel to speculate about what it means to write as the daughter of such mothers. . . . Does Woolf's

130

idea of a woman's art require the death of the mother? Or does it rather depend on her continued life? In particular, Woolf asks, does representation require the mother's death, making non-representational art preferable? Or can representation be reclaimed for mothers and daughters?

Like [George Eliot's] Romola,[4] Mrs Ramsay is an ideally beautiful Madonna figure. For Mr Bankes, watching Lily paint them, she and her son amount to 'mother and child then – objects of universal veneration' (*To the Lighthouse*, p. 59). Like Romola reading to her father and to her stepson stories endorsing the exclusion of women, she reads to James a story about the dangers of women's desires. She selflessly tends her family and the poor and sick, and she too serves an egotistical scholar. In this role, Mrs Ramsay arouses both scepticism and admiration . . . .

As a mother, however, Mrs Ramsay also embodies both Western culture's fear of the mother who is identified with nature and the literal and some daughters' rebellious love of this mother. Her civilising work – the creation of the house and of the social relations that thrive there – is destroyed by nature in 'Time Passes', yet she is also a 'rosy-flowered fruit tree laid with leaves and dancing boughs' (p. 44). As Maria DiBattista argues, she is identified, through 'this mania of hers for marriage' (p. 190) and reproduction, with the vitality and the relentless forces of nature.[5] And as Gayatri Spivak points out, Mrs Ramsay sees the marriages she sponsors as specifically continuing her maternal line.[6] Paradoxically, her matchmaking and her association with nature make her both the Angel in the House and her reverse . . . . The history of her daughter Prue most succinctly exposes the ambiguity of the appeal for her daughters of Mrs Ramsay's alliance with nature. Aspiring to repeat her mother's life, Prue reproduces only a reduced version of her mother's reproductive history, because for Prue, as for Cathy [in Emily Brontë's *Wuthering Heights*[7]], childbirth leads directly to death. As a figure for Mother Nature, Mrs Ramsay summarises both the nature that Cathy suicidally loves and remains loyal to and the nature that Lockwood [in *Wuthering Heights*] and Jane Eyre[8] fear. She is both the loved body of a daughter's mother and the feared body of a son's (or male-identified daughter's) mother.

Through this woman with her 'core of darkness' (p. 69), Woolf reconsiders the Victorian novel's ambivalence about the possibility that the mother is beyond or prior to language. This is clear, for example, in 'The Window', which ends with her triumphant resistance to speech:

> He wanted something – wanted the thing she always found it so difficult to give him; wanted her to tell him that she loved him. And that, no, she could not do. . . . As she looked at him she began to smile, for though she had not said a word, he knew, of course he knew, that she loved him. He could not deny it. And smiling she looked out of the window and said (thinking to herself, Nothing on earth can equal this happiness) –
> 'Yes, you were right. It's going to be wet tomorrow. You won't be able to go.' And she looked at him smiling. For she had triumphed again. She had not said it: yet he knew.⁹

Perhaps . . . she deludes herself in thinking that by depriving herself of language she has gained her power over him, for she 'triumphs' only while speaking words that concede his real authority over nature and over her. On the other hand, Woolf makes it equally possible that this is a genuine triumph. If words distance their referents, then not to represent her love is to keep it present and alive. Her inconsequential words, which bear so slight and tangential a relation to her thought, operate like the words she shares with Cam after the dinner party (pp. 124–5): they resist representation and instead create a present relation. She stands for both the danger and the value of a woman's adherence to the literal. Like Molly Gibson's dead mother and Mrs Hamley in *Wives and Daughters*,¹⁰ she initially authorises a daughter's non-symbolic discourse yet offers her a deceptive promise, for the mother–daughter relation was from the beginning incorporated within the law. Mrs Ramsay talks Cam to sleep as movingly and subversively as she does only because she has yielded to James's fetishisation of the horned skull, just as the first Mrs Gibson and as Mrs Hamley authorise a language whose function is to transmit men's words.

The novel constructs its paradigms of the relation of a daughter's art to the mother on all these ambiguous aspects of Mrs Ramsay. We will begin by looking at Cam's relation to language as a story about the daughter as an artist, since it was with her exchange with Mrs Ramsay that we initially posited a mother–daughter language existing outside the law of representation.¹¹ Because 'she and James shared the same tastes' (p. 62), Mrs Ramsay welcomes the departure of 'that wild villain, Cam' (p. 60) when she is reading to James. Yet although Mrs Ramsay . . . in this way identifies her interests as a narrator with those of patriarchy, she also understands and sympathises with her daughter: she invites Cam to leave, 'knowing that Cam was attracted only by the word "Flounder"' (p. 62). Like other daughters who live outside the law – notably the first Cathy, the second Cathy as a child [in *Wuthering Heights*], [Mrs Gaskell's] Lizzie Leigh[12] – she loves the sounds of words for themselves, especially in so far as they guarantee the mother's presence. It is this understanding that Mrs Ramsay again displays when she talks her daughter to sleep after the dinner party. Another scene recalls and reverses the scene of the second Cathy's entry into the law: Cam 'was picking Sweet Alice on the bank. She was wild and fierce. She would not "give a flower to the gentleman" as the nursemaid told her. No! no! no! she would not! She clenched her fist. She stamped' (p. 26). [In *Wuthering Heights*] Cathy Linton at age seventeen won't pick a flower because she has learned to read nature symbolically;[13] Cam picks flowers but, herself interchangeable with flowers bearing a girl's name, refuses to bend either nature or herself to a man's will.

'That wild villain, Cam, dashing past' (p. 60) reincarnates not only one of 'the Kings and Queens of England; Cam the Wicked' (p. 26), but also Virgil's Camilla, the warrior whose history is recounted and who dies fighting against Aeneas in Book XI of *The Aeneid*. Camilla's most striking feature is her speed:

> If she ran full speed
> Over the tips of grain unharvested
> She would not ever have bruised an ear, or else
> She might have sprinted on the deep sea swell
> And never dipped her flying feet.[14]

Of her own speeding outlaw Woolf writes,

> Cam grazed the easel by an inch; . . . she would not stop for her father, whom she grazed also by an inch; nor for her mother, who called 'Cam! I want you a moment!' as she dashed past. She was off like a bird, bullet, or arrow, impelled by what desire, shot by whom, at what directed, who could say? What, what? Mrs Ramsay pondered, watching her. It might be a vision – of a shell, of a wheelbarrow, of a fairy kingdom on the far side of the hedge; or it might be the glory of speed; no one knew.
>
> (pp. 60–1)

When the motherless Camilla was a child, her father saved her life by binding her to a spear and hurling her across a river; Woolf continues, 'But when Mrs Ramsay called "Cam!" a second time, the projectile dropped in mid career, and Cam came lagging back, pulling a leaf by the way, to her mother' (p. 61). Both Cam and Camilla are 'projectiles', yet where Camilla is hurled by her father, Cam is impelled by an unrepresentable force, and ends with her mother. Reluctant to join a mother who represents the law, Cam also knows her mother's sympathy with female outlawry.

Virgil has his Camilla die of 'a girl's love of finery': she is distracted in battle by her desire for an enemy's beautiful clothes, succumbing like Dorothea Brooke [in the first chapter of *Middlemarch*[15]] to the beauty of her mother's jewels, as if the mother's heritage were only the trivia of decoration. Woolf, by contrast, values and so redefines the mother's heritage, allowing Cam's return to her mother to be played out at the end of the novel in a highly favourable way. Toward the end of the voyage, Cam, looking back at the distant, small island, sleepily repeats to herself the words her mother spoke after the dinner party:

> All those paths and terraces and bedrooms were fading and disappearing, and nothing was left but a pale blue censer swinging rhythmically this way and that across her mind. It was a hanging garden; it was a valley, full of birds, and flowers, and antelopes. . . . She was falling asleep.
>
> (p. 221)[16]

Cam has not lost her childhood 'parrot-like instinct' to repeat words 'in a colourless singsong' (p. 61). This reproduction of her mother's words marks a turning point in the voyage, for it is when Cam wakes up in the next paragraph that Mr Ramsay has changed from mournful romantic quester to distributor of sandwiches. Although she earlier in the voyage also repeats her father's words – 'she murmured, dreamily half asleep, how we perished, each alone' (p. 207) – and although she yields to her father's demand for her sympathy, the mother has the last word. In the masculine, military world of *The Aeneid*, to choose the mother is to die (as it would be also in *Jane Eyre*, when Jane is tempted to seek the embrace of Mother Nature[17]), while in Woolf's novel a girl can choose to remain the daughter of her mother, to repeat her, and stay alive.

What does it mean for Cam to repeat her mother's words in this way? [In the original passage[18]] 'valleys and flowers and bells ringing and birds singing and little goats and antelopes' (*To the Lighthouse*, p. 124) did not signify referential objects (either the antelopes they seem to denominate or the boar's skull for which they appear to be metaphors) but rather constituted a link, through non-representational sounds, between the mother's body and the daughter's. That Cam repeats these words with reference to an entirely different object, the distant island, confirms that they are non-representational: they have as little to do with an island as with any other referent, for their function is instead comfortingly to recall the mother. And Cam succeeds, for the spirit of Mrs Ramsay now appears to enter the boat and join her husband.

But Cam is not the artist in the novel, and it is not her relation to language and the mother that the novel adduces as its principal paradigm for its own practice. We will want to consider why, after taking a look at the complex relation between Lily Briscoe's art and the life and death of so ambiguous a mother as Mrs Ramsay. While Mr Bankes sees Mrs Ramsay as the Madonna, Lily shocks him by reducing 'the significance of mother and son' to a purple shadow, to an effect of 'how a light there needed a shadow there' (p. 191). Compared to Mr Bankes's notion of art, Lily's picture does not victimise Mrs Ramsay through representation: 'But the picture was not of them, she said' (p. 59). It takes the mother and child as its pretext, but it does not freeze them as a representational painting would, and especially it does not subordinate Mrs Ramsay to the Christian denial, through the notion of Mary's virginity, of the mother's body. After Mrs Ramsay's death, Mr Ramsay will accept almost any woman as a substitute for her: indiscriminately, he demands sympathy from all the women in his vicinity, even from Lily, who resembles Mrs Ramsay solely in gender. Women are for Mr Ramsay . . . a signifying chain, and one will do almost as well as another. His loss only confirms and darkens his role as romantic quester ('we perished, each alone' [p. 180]). By contrast, Lily responds to Mrs Ramsay's death by really wanting her, and only her, back again. For her, Mrs Ramsay is irreplaceable, and representation is wholly inadequate for the purposes of recovering her.

> Little words that broke up the thought and dismembered it said nothing. . . . Words fluttered sideways and struck the object inches too low. . . . For how could one express in words these emotions of the body? express that emptiness there? (She was looking at the drawing-room steps; they looked extraordinarily empty.) It was one's body feeling, not one's mind. The physical sensations that went with the bare look of the steps had become suddenly extremely unpleasant. To want and not to have, sent all up her body a hardness, a hollowness,

a strain. And then to want and not to have – to want and want – how that wrung the heart, and wrung it again and again! Oh, Mrs Ramsay! she called out silently.

(pp. 193–4)

That Lily, in contrast to Mr Ramsay, experiences Mrs Ramsay's loss with such particularity and as a physical sensation exemplifies the difference we have hypothesised between a daughter's and a son's relation to the mother: Lily wants to reproduce her, and wants to reproduce a relation to a present body, while Mr Ramsay wants to replace or represent her.

This difference leads us to expect that Lily's art would seek not to represent but rather to reproduce Mrs Ramsay. But Lily's paintings are as different from Cam's reproduction of her mother's non-representational words as they are from the Raphael Madonnas that Mr Bankes has in mind. The shapes on Lily's canvas do not represent Mrs Ramsay in any conventional sense, but they do represent the shapes of light and shadow made by Mrs Ramsay's body. Quite possibly, Woolf wants us to see that Lily's painting is representational, if only in a subtler way than Raphael's. She does not simply create abstract patterns on her canvas; she paints out of doors and she is irritated if something or someone changes the composition that she is painting. Moreover, when Lily paints in Mrs Ramsay's presence, she is unable to complete her painting; only after Mrs Ramsay's death does she manage to finish successfully. What most tellingly distinguishes Cam from Lily is that Lily's art still depends upon memory. While Cam in her inability to remember the points of the compass reproduces Mrs Ramsay (Mr Ramsay thinks, 'It had been so with her – his wife. They could not keep anything clearly fixed in their minds' [p. 182]), Lily's second painting does require the memory of the mother and therefore her absence. Just as Lily must reject Mrs Ramsay's Victorian values and her beauty, it is only through her efforts to remember Mrs Ramsay that she can solve the problem of her picture. 'She went on tunnelling her way into her picture, into the past. . . . So much depends, she thought, upon distance' (pp. 188, 207). In the course of remembering Mrs Ramsay, Lily thinks, 'she did not want Mrs Ramsay now' (p. 212), for her memory substitutes fullness for emptiness. When Lily sees the phantom kitchen table lodged in the fork of the pear tree at the beginning of the novel, she does . . . restore the mother's presence, but only relatively.[19] Her vision in a different sense depends on the referent's absence, for . . .

she superimposes her projection onto the present reality of the tree. When the phantom Mrs Ramsay, 'a sense of someone there', appears in response to Lily's crying out her name, as much as it may inscribe a new and female kind of restoration, it may equally reinscribe the romantic pattern, the return as figuration of 'someone like the mother'. If Lily's art is modelled on a son's, then Lily's version of Mrs Ramsay is indeed Madonna-like, for the final form of her angelic selflessness is her death, which makes possible the completion of a work of art.[20] Having coaxed the daughter by the seductive promise of her own presence into serving instead the father, Mrs Ramsay vanishes, leaving an absence on which a work of art may be constructed. Cam's repetition of her mother's words reproduces her by placing Cam in her mother's place, speaking with her words, while Lily's project inevitably courts the dangers of representation. As in *Wuthering Heights*, the daughter who is most fiercely loyal to the mother is also the least likely to be or to stand for the artist.

Woolf's own practice in writing the novel shares the ambiguities of Lily's art. Although *To the Lighthouse* seems to favour the possibilities of non-representational art and holds out the possibility that Lily's painting avoids at least some of the pitfalls of representation, we cannot see the painting. (Did Woolf make her artist figure a painter and not a poet so as to make it impossible for her art to enter the boundaries of the novel?) What Woolf provides instead is a representational account of the painting, together with Lily's reconstruction of Mrs Ramsay through the representational words of her memory. And Lily's long retrospect occupies far more of the novel's time than does the account of her painting. Moreover, her retrospect is synonymous with Woolf's: writing an elegy for her parents, Woolf, like Lily, creates a fullness with memory that depends upon the parents' deaths. It is well known that in a quite literal sense Woolf felt her becoming a writer at all depended on the deaths of parents whose lives told her, in different ways, as Charles Tansley tells Lily, 'Women can't paint, women can't write' (*To the Lighthouse*, p. 54).

Why does Woolf persist in the representational project? Why doesn't she go beyond the linguistic practice that she criticises? Why can't Cam's way with words, instead of Lily's, model the novelist's own practice? Perhaps the situation is a consequence of her writing a novel about the Victorian family. It may be that Woolf embodies her criticism of the Victorian family – and of its effects on its daughters – in the effect it has on her own practice, by having such a family produce such a relation to language. . . . For Cam to repeat her mother's words may embody a revolutionary and potentially anti-patriarchal way of using language, . . . [but it also means she repeats] her mother's submissiveness toward Mr Ramsay. . . . If Cam's ability to reproduce her mother tongue ends only in her becoming an Angel in the House, then the promise for liberating women's language that this mother–daughter language seemed to hold out will not, after all, have been fulfilled. As when she has Minta Doyle leave *Middlemarch* on the train (*To the Lighthouse*, p. 91), Woolf resents and distances the mother's Victorian legacy, while she also attempts to revalue and recover a different maternal heritage, the mother's body and the new relations its presence makes possible.

From Margaret Homans, *Bearing the Word. Language and Female Experience in Nineteenth-Century Women's Writing* (Chicago and London, 1986), pp. 278–87.

NOTES

[This essay is taken from the 'Postscript' of Margaret Homans's book. In extracting it from the original slightly longer chapter I have omitted passages at the beginning and end which link it specifically to the rest of the book, and I have made changes of detail, especially in the first and last paragraphs here, which were kindly suggested by Professor Homans herself.

The essay is concerned to demonstrate Woolf's ambivalence about the maternal heritage of a woman writer. Its argument rests on a distinction made in some psychoanalytic theory between two uses of language. One of these uses is as a survival between mothers and daughters of bodily communication between them. This is called 'literal' language because it asserts the actual physical presence of the mother. In contrast is the 'symbolic' use of language, the use sanctioned by public communication. Here the words predominantly refer to, or 'mean', something other than themselves. In effect, they represent or symbolise the things to which they refer, and so always stand in the place of something which is absent. The word 'mother' is not itself mother: it is a sign in place of her.

Early in her book (pp. 16–21) Homans discusses the scene in *To the Lighthouse* in which Mrs Ramsay, after the dinner party, covers the sheep's skull in her children's bedroom with her shawl, and talks differently about this to Cam and to James (*To the Lighthouse*, pp. 124–5). To Cam her words convey the mother's soothing presence, and any other reference or meaning they might carry is irrelevant. Homans says that in this way the novel asserts 'a myth of a daughter's never having lost the literal language she shared with her mother' (p. 18). But alongside this, the words to James operate symbolically: they indicate to him that something he can no longer see, the skull, still exists and can be thought of.

Homans (*Bearing the Word*, pp. 18–19) opposes this idea of 'literal' maternal language to Julia Kristeva's idea of a disruptive 'semiotic' language which is a return to a 'forbidden' maternal body; she argues that while the mother–daughter language of infancy is indeed *suppressed* by social custom it is not *repressed*. She goes on (pp. 19–20) to argue that whenever Woolf constructs examples of this mother–daughter language she also perpetuates its suppression because she only represents it within symbolic language: she does not actually write it. In this essay, at the end of her book and after discussing various Victorian women novelists, Homans uses Cam and, especially, Lily to argue that in Woolf's work a woman writer or artist must still suppress the literal language of her mother and use the symbolic instead.

Readers should compare this essay with Elizabeth Abel's (p. 112 above). That makes a different use of psychoanalytic theory and concludes, in contrast, that Cam represents the loss, not the perpetuation, of the mother–daughter language of babyhood, and that it is through Lily Briscoe that the novel offers an image of a feminine language.

As throughout this volume, references to *To the Lighthouse* are to the Penguin edition with Introduction and Notes by Hermione Lee and text edited by Stella McNichol (London, 1992), except when it is indicated otherwise. Professor Homans's original essay refers to the American edition, published in New York in 1927 by Harcourt Brace. One of her quotations differs from the Penguin edition (see note 9 below). Ed.]

1. Virginia Woolf, *A Room of One's Own* (London, 1929; Penguin edition 1945, 1992), p. 76.

2. Jane Marcus, 'Liberty, Sorority, Misogyny', in Carolyn G. Heilbrun and Margaret R. Higonnet (eds), *The Representation of Women in Fiction* (Baltimore, 1983), p. 71.

3. [Michèle Barrett (ed.), *Virginia Woolf, Women and Writing* (London, 1979), pp. 58, 59, 60. Woolf's essay 'Professions for Women' was first published in *The Death of the Moth and Other Essays* (London, 1942) but an earlier longer version, a typescript for a speech given in 1931, is in *The Pargiters. The Novel-Essay Portion of The Years*, ed. Mitchell A. Leaska (London, 1978), pp. xxvii–xliv. Ed.]

4. George Eliot, *Romola*, 1863.

5. Maria DiBattista, *Virginia Woolf's Major Novels: The Fables of Anon* (New Haven, 1980), p. 75. Geoffrey Hartman also points out that Mrs Ramsay is associated with 'the will of nature', both with natural vitality and with nature's destructiveness (see 'Virginia's Web', in his *Beyond Formalism* [New Haven, 1970], p. 82). Avrom Fleishman likewise sees Mrs Ramsay as an ambiguous queen, with powers both benign and sinister (*Virginia Woolf: A Critical Reading* [Baltimore and London, 1975], pp. 109–10, 157).

6. Gayatri Spivak, 'Making and Unmaking in *To the Lighthouse*', in Sally McConnell-Ginet, Ruth Borker and Nelly Furman (eds), *Women and Language in Literature and Society* (New York, 1980), p. 315.

7. Emily Brontë, *Wuthering Heights*, 1847.

8. Charlotte Brontë, *Jane Eyre*, 1847.

9. [This quotation is taken from the American edition published in New York in 1927 by Harcourt Brace, pp. 184–6. The British edition reads: '"Yes, you were right. It's going to be wet tomorrow." She had not said it, but he knew it. And she looked at him smiling. For she had triumphed again' (Penguin edn, 1992, p. 134). Ed.]

10. Elizabeth Gaskell, *Wives and Daughters: An Everyday Story*, 1866.

11. Homans, *Bearing the Word*, pp. 17–20.

12. Elizabeth Gaskell, *Lizzie Leigh and Other Tales*, 1855.

13. [Earlier in her book Homans discusses a scene in Chapter 22 of *Wuthering Heights*: here the second Cathy, who is about to be removed from childhood into the adult world by the death of her father and by the power of Heathcliff, refuses to pick a bluebell and, Homans suggests, 'gives it a meaning, as adults do: "No, I'll not touch it – but it looks melancholy, does it not?"' (Homans, *Bearing the Word*, p. 75). Ed.]

14. Virgil, *The Aeneid*, trans. Robert Fitzgerald (New York, 1983), p. 225.

15. George Eliot, *Middlemarch. A Study of Provincial Life*, 1874.

16. I am grateful to Maria DiBattista for pointing out to me the significance of this passage for my argument.

17. [As in Jane's flight from Rochester. Homans (*Bearing the Word*, p. 93) quotes from Chapter 28 of *Jane Eyre*: 'I have no relative but the universal mother, Nature: I will seek her breast and ask repose.' Homans argues (pp. 84–99) that *Jane Eyre* demonstrates the knowledge that the desire to return to the mother is, in spite of its attraction, inimical to the aims of the novelist. Ed.]

18. [Early in her book (*Bearing the Word*, pp. 16–21) Professor Homans discusses the scene in which Mrs Ramsay hides the sheep's skull in the children's bedroom with her shawl and then talks to each child, differently, about it (*To the Lighthouse*, pp. 124–5). She argues that Mrs Ramsay's words to James signify a meaning, being designed to tell him that the skull is there although no longer seen; but that her words to Cam, in contrast, enact her own physical presence. Ed.]

19. [At the beginning of her book (*Bearing the Word*, pp. 1–2) Homans has argued that Lily's image for his work mocks Mr Ramsay's abstract philosophy with the presence of a kitchen table and, beside it, a maternal figure. Ed.]

20. As DiBattista writes in *Virginia Woolf's Major Novels, To the Lighthouse* 'concerns itself with the death of the beloved queen mother and her resurrection through art' (p. 93). She also argues that 'the novel is an elegiac narrative that treats its subject – the dead mother and father – exclusively in terms of the surviving daughter, the implied, anonymous narrator of the novel' (p. 68). Agreeing with DiBattista, I place these insights in a different context to give them an added significance. Susan Dick also argues for the importance of memory in the novel, and particularly in Lily's painting, in 'The Tunnelling Process: Some Aspects of Virginia Woolf's Use of Memory and the Past', in Patricia Clements and Isobel Grundy (eds), *Virginia Woolf: New Critical Essays* (London, 1983), pp. 190–5. John Mepham discusses Woolf's own comments about the novel as the completion of her mourning for her mother and as an elegy in 'Mourning and Modernism' also in Clements and Grundy (eds), *Virginia Woolf: New Critical Essays*, p. 142.

10

Thinking Forward Through Mrs Dalloway's Daughter

RACHEL BOWLBY

How far have women come? To answer such a question, it would be necessary to establish where women meant or were meant to go, to know their destination, and that of feminism. In *Three Guineas*, notoriously, Woolf looks forward at one point to a time when the word 'feminist' will have ceased to exist. In the context, the concern is with 'the right to earn a living':[1] at the end of the line, feminism has done its work when women have become eligible to enter the professions on the same basis as men. But elsewhere, it is not at all clear what for Woolf would constitute the 'end' of feminism: its purpose or its dissolution, as the movement reaches its goal.

* * *

[Three paragraphs in the original essay, omitted here, discuss Woolf's 'equivocations' on issues of what women's aims and destinations should be, and suggest that *Mrs Dalloway* foregrounds many of these issues. Ed.]

When Elizabeth Dalloway steps out and takes the bus up the Strand on a fine June day in 1923, everything seems to suggest that she is the bearer of new opportunities for her sex, a woman who will be able to go further than her mother, still bound to the conventional femininity of the Victorian Angel in the House denounced by Woolf in 'Professions for Women'.[2] Elizabeth indulges in an excursion of independent fancy through the streets of London during which she is associated with the omnipotence attributed to the means of transport:

142

> Suddenly Elizabeth stepped forward and most competently boarded
> the omnibus, in front of everybody. She took a seat on top. The
> impetuous creature – a pirate – started forward, sprang away; she had
> to hold the rail to steady herself, for a pirate it was, reckless,
> unscrupulous, bearing down ruthlessly, circumventing dangerously,
> boldly snatching a passenger, or ignoring a passenger, squeezing eel-
> like and arrogant in between, and then rushing insolently all sails
> spread up Whitehall.
>
> (*Mrs Dalloway*, p. 148)

The movement through unfamiliar parts of the city inspires Elizabeth
with ideas of a life quite different from that of her mother, criticised
by Peter Walsh as 'the perfect hostess' (p. 67):

> Oh, she would like to go a little farther. Another penny, was it, to the
> Strand? Here was another penny, then. She would go up the Strand.
>   She liked people who were ill. And every profession is open to the
> women of your generation, said Miss Kilman. So she might be a
> doctor. She might be a farmer. . . . It was quite different here from
> Westminster, she thought, getting off at Chancery Lane. It was so
> serious; it was so busy. In short, she would like to have a profession.
> She would become a doctor, a farmer, possibly go into Parliament if
> she found it necessary, all because of the Strand.
>
> (*Mrs Dalloway*, p. 149)

Elizabeth's imaginative venture could be taken as a positive sign of
women's progress: she is driven by ambitions beyond the ken of
women thirty years before, and unencumbered by the pressure of
masculine interference. Rather, in that she may become an MP, like
Richard Dalloway, she identifies with the possibilities of a paternal
profession.

No bar is placed on her rambling exploration, which suggests a
difference from a related Victorian text which is cited, and censured,
in *A Room of One's Own*. 'That is an awkward break', announces
the edgy narrator,[3] who wishes that what seems to be Grace Poole's
laugh did not intrude upon what then seems all the more defensive a
protest on behalf of women's 'restlessness' and right to wider experience. The chapter of *Jane Eyre* from which Woolf quotes begins
with the optimistic statement that 'The promise of a smooth career,
which my first introduction to Thornfield Hall seemed to pledge, was
not belied on a longer acquaintance with the place and its inmates',[4]
but the limits to the satisfaction afforded by that career appear on the
very same page:

I longed for a power of vision which might overpass that limit; which might reach the busy world, towns, regions full of life I had heard of but never seen; . . . I desired more of practical experience than I possessed. . . .

Who blames me? Many, no doubt, and I shall be called discontented. I could not help it; the restlessness was in my nature; it agitated me to pain sometimes. Then my sole relief was to walk along the corridor of the third storey, backwards and forwards, safe in the silence and solitude of the spot, and allow my mind's eye to dwell on whatever bright visions rose before it – and, certainly, they were many and glowing; to let my heart be heaved by the exultant movement, which, while it swelled it in trouble, expanded it with life; and, best of all, to open my inward ear to a tale that was never ended – a tale my imagination created, and narrated continuously; quickened with all of incident, life, fire, feeling, that I desired and had not in my actual existence.[5]

Woolf's own citation of the passage beginning 'Who blames me?' breaks off awkwardly after 'pain sometimes'. The focus is then on a 'restlessness' detached from both the desire for 'practical' experience and sights of 'the busy world', and the imaginary 'relief' of the 'bright visions' and the 'tale that was never ended', supplying 'all of incident, life, fire, feeling' missing in actuality.

It is these omissions which make possible Woolf's criticism of gratuitous expressions of anger by women writers. But it is as if the eliminated parts return in Woolf's own novel to structure her twentieth-century rewriting of the Victorian spinster's prospects, where every element is included *except* the anger. For Elizabeth Dalloway there is no censorious Beadle or Woolf to put a stop to her reverie. A practical aspect to her dreams is suggested in the repeated, tangible fact that women can now enter the professions: Elizabeth is presumably in no danger of having to become an impecunious orphan governess, *à la* Jane Eyre, and thus (in Woolf's terms) has no need to give vent to the anger condemned as a flaw in her predecessor. So it might indeed seem that what was mere fantasy for a nineteenth-century woman, an imagining of liberty so futile as to be psychologically debilitating, has now become a realistic possibility. Whereas Jane Eyre dreams out from a distant rural rooftop, Elizabeth Dalloway is already on top of the bus, travelling through the city in which she may well fulfil her ambitions.

This point could be reinforced by placing Elizabeth's London adventure alongside that of another Brontë heroine, Lucy Snowe. On her way to be a teacher in Villette in Belgium, Lucy stops for a night in London and explores the City with the same passion that grips her twentieth-century literary descendant:

> Descending, I went wandering whither chance might lead, in a still ecstacy of freedom and enjoyment; and I got – I know not how – I got into the heart of city life. I saw and felt London at last: I got into the Strand; I went up Cornhill; I mixed with the life passing along; I dared the perils of crossings. To do this, and to do it utterly alone, gave me, perhaps an irrational, but a real pleasure. Since those days, I have seen the West-end, the parks, the fine squares; but I love the city far better. The city seems to me so much more in earnest: its business, its rush, its roar, are such serious things, sights, and sounds. The city is getting its living – the West-end but enjoying its pleasure.[6]

Lucy makes the same distinction as Elizabeth between the 'serious' city business of 'getting a living' and the relative triviality of other parts: 'the West-end *but* enjoying its pleasure'. Like Elizabeth, she travels at random, 'whither chance might lead'; and for Lucy too, the solitary discovery of unknown regions is itself 'a real pleasure'.

Yet further on, crossing the Channel, she will correct her sunny speculations about a European future 'grand with imperial promise' for herself:

> Cancel the whole of that, if you please, reader – or rather let it stand, and draw thence a moral – an alternative, text-hand copy –
> Day-dreams are delusions of the demon.[7]

And previously, the decision to venture was represented as anything but a wide open prospect:

> A strong, vague persuasion, that it was better to go forward than backward, and that I *could* go forward – that a way, however narrow and difficult, would in time open, predominated over other feelings: its influence hushed them so far, that at last I became sufficiently tranquil to be able to say my prayers and seek my couch.[8]

Lucy's humble future in Villette is more a response to necessity than the fulfilment of a far-flung desire for a wider experience, the 'day-dreams' whose dangerous and unsettling effects must be censored for the sake of sanity.

The apparent contrast in the outlooks of Brontë governesses and Dalloway daughters is reinforced by a difference of social class. The penniless Jane Eyre and Lucy Snowe do what is decently possible and financially unavoidable for the respectable poor; Elizabeth Dalloway comes of Establishment stock, and has herself been educated by an impoverished exile. This is the formidable Miss Kilman, who has had none of her pupil's chances, and whose bitterness is perhaps, by caricature, another Woolfian jab at the anger of the Brontë heroine. It is as if Miss Kilman is a nineteenth-century specimen rudely repackaged and sent on, complete with a religious faith whose anachronism in the secular Dalloway society is underlined by its fundamentalist excess. Such a character, like the suffrage workers of *Night and Day* and like 'Miss Julia Hedge, the feminist' in *Jacob's Room*, is one of a fairly numerous sisterhood in Woolf's novels.[9]

But these complexities should already suggest that the passage from the nineteenth to the twentieth century is not so direct or progressive as it may at first have seemed. For while Elizabeth Dalloway's daydreams are certainly more realisable in one sense than Lucy Snowe's or Jane Eyre's, they are no less marked, like Jane Eyre's, by a fantasy of transgression, which is set in a close relation to the various familial and educational influences on her.

The bus trip is initially an escape from the by now unbearable company of the same Miss Kilman who is the origin of her ideas of female aspiration. But Elizabeth's attachment to her, and in particular this afternoon's outing which began as a visit to the Army and Navy Stores, is in part in defiance of her mother, to whom it is a cause of distress. Professional plans are explicitly conceived as anti-maternal: she is 'quite determined, whatever her mother might say, to become either a farmer or a doctor' (*Mrs Dalloway*, p. 150). And this despite the fact that her mother apparently considers the idea of Dalloway professional women as a long-established tradition, not a revolutionary breakthrough or breaking away:

> But then, of course, there was in the Dalloway family the tradition of public service. Abbesses, principals, head mistresses, dignitaries, in the republic of women – without being brilliant, any of them, they were that.
>
> (p. 150)

For Clarissa, female authority is a matter 'of course'. Elizabeth's professional fantasy is thus ironic in that it functions as an escape from what she perceives as the constraints of two supporters of professions for women, the mother and the governess. And Elizabeth readily returns for the time being to her domestic calling as a good, civilised daughter: 'She must go home. She must dress for dinner. But what was the time? – where was a clock?' (p. 150). The novel's finale places her at the side of her father, with whose professional achievements she earlier courted an identification. Now, instead, she is seen by him, unrecognised at first, as a beautiful young woman. This does not make her her father's equal or surrogate, but effectively returns her to the position of the idealised object of what she dismissed before as 'trivial chatterings (comparing women to poplar trees)' (p. 150).

Elizabeth's destiny, then, is far from certain in either its evaluation or its outcome. Her predicament places her alternatives as between the possibility of participation in the centres of masculine power, as 'unscrupulous' and 'arrogant' as the bus (p. 148), and what appears as an ignominious succumbing to a 'trivial' femininity as the object of male admiration. The incompatibility of the two is pathetically suggested by the scene of Miss Kilman's resentful and random purchase of a petticoat in the department store.

But Elizabeth's story is not, of course, the primary focus of *Mrs Dalloway*. That is part of what makes it so innovative a text, in that the heroine is the woman of fifty and not her eighteen-year-old daughter on the brink of courtship. For the most visible subject of the novel is the insistent re-enactment for the older woman of the romantic drama which according to most of literature should have been 'settled' once and for all thirty years before, with her choice of Richard Dalloway as a husband.

In a stimulating essay on *Mrs Dalloway*, Elizabeth Abel says that the novel 'demonstrates the common literary prefiguration of psychoanalytic doctrine, which can retroactively articulate patterns implicit in the literary text'.[10] Recapitulating the difficulty of the development towards 'normal' heterosexual femininity as described by Freud, Abel reads the conclusion as Clarissa's belated acceptance, thirty years after the events, of her 'choice' of Richard over the pre-Oedipal female bonding of her relationship with Sally Seton.

The particular inflection in *Mrs Dalloway* of such a claim for the prefiguring of psychoanalytic theories can be pointed up, once again, by a comparison with Brontë. In *Villette*, there is a literal recovery of the original family setting when Lucy Snowe awakens after her lapse of consciousness to find herself once again surrounded by the relatives familiar from her childhood, magically removed to the same foreign city; which then leads to the beginning of what she imagines as a romantic relationship with her attractive male cousin. In *Mrs Dalloway*, such a structure is reinscribed in the form of the literal reappearance of many of the chief and minor actors in the decisive period of Clarissa's youth: Ellie Henderson, Aunt Helena – 'for Miss Helena Parry was not dead' (p. 195) – Sally Seton, and above all Peter Walsh. Yet this functions not as a new start in the form of new romantic commitments, but as a means of negotiating what are shown to have been insistently present rememberings of that time in the minds of Clarissa and Peter throughout the day and, by implication, throughout their lives.

Sally's passionate kiss, interrupted by Peter and another man, is centred in Abel's reading as representing the impossible and abandoned alternative to the nun-like chastity Clarissa has instead adopted in becoming Mrs Richard Dalloway. Her daughter's liaison with Doris Kilman, in contrast, is a more ambivalent female bonding, since it is described in terms of conflicting determinations and structured in relation to a revolt from her own mother, the first, and female, object of love. The 'purity' (p. 37) of the relationship with Sally stands out all the more by comparison; but it is so in virtue of its status as a memory, an old wives' tale which figures in retrospect for Clarissa as the lost idyll of youth before she married and moved to London. What the novel suggests, then, is not so much the purer status of love between women as the giving up implicit in the turn to maturity, in this case heterosexual. For as Abel points out, Clarissa's feelings for women are themselves infiltrated by masculine and feminine imagery: 'she did undoubtedly then feel what men felt' (p. 34).

Peter Walsh also features in Clarissa's reminiscences (as she in his), representing the romantic hero rejected in favour of the conventionality personified by the Conservative Member of Parliament.[11] She reacts after Peter's unexpected morning visit:

> If I had married him, this gaiety would have been mine all day!
> It was all over for her. The sheet was stretched and the bed narrow. She had gone up into the tower alone and left them blackberrying in the sun.
>
> (p. 51)

Again, it is not so much implied that Clarissa should have married Peter really, as that the choice of a life as Mrs Dalloway made way for the idealisation of the two other lovers thereby given up: that it was not a one-and-only choice and as a result has been written over, throughout its long duration, with memories and imaginings of the other lives neglected for that of the 'perfect hostess'.

The instabilities and overlappings of individual identity are constantly, repeatedly emphasised in *Mrs Dalloway*. Clarissa herself 'would not say of any one in the world now that they were this or were that' (p. 8); the ending, with her reaction to the suicide of a man she has never heard of, reinforces a connection that the narrative, with its separate account of the drama of Septimus and Lucrezia Warren Smith, has implicitly made all along. Her objection, in the same context, to the psychiatrist's doctrine of 'Proportion' ('Sir William said he never spoke of "madness"; he called it not having a sense of proportion' [p. 106]) parallels Septimus' own.

The lack of settlement or of fixed identity in Clarissa's life stands out also in its difference from the order and regularity – the daily 'proportions' – indicated by the repeated chiming of Big Ben. The intoning of the hours is associated with the authority of national and other institutions: with what Paul Ricoeur, following Nietzsche, calls 'monumental' time.[12] Ricoeur links this with the symbolic force of the figure of royalty passing in anonymous majesty through London during Clarissa's shopping expedition; or with the enigmatically suggestive advertising slogan written on high and eagerly deciphered by the crowd whom it equally draws together and hails from the sky with its brand-name riddle.

Such emblems of power are fully implicated in this novel, as habitually in Woolf, with masculinity institutionalised and imposing. Here Peter Walsh looks on:

> Boys in uniform, carrying guns, marched with their eyes ahead of them, marched, their arms stiff, and on their faces an expression like the letters of a legend written round the base of a statue praising duty, gratitude, fidelity, love of England.
>
> (p. 55)

Big Ben keeps in time with this lifeless national parade of conformity and 'discipline' (p. 56):

> The sound of Big Ben striking the half-hour struck out between them with extraordinary vigour, as if a young man, strong, indifferent, inconsiderate, were swinging dumb-bells this way and that.
>
> (p. 52)

It is as if the highlighting of the time, almost a refrain with the repetition in the narrative of exact forms of words, brings to the fore the artifice of the naturalised structure within which individual lives and times are differentiated. A similar effect is produced in *The Waves* by the poetic interludes describing the movement of the sun, and making the analogy between a life, or six lives, and a day. But whereas that time is represented as the natural framework of a recurring solar movement, in *Mrs Dalloway* the use of the clock and the specification of hours and half hours proceeding in order from one to twelve and from a.m. to p.m. makes time more linear than circular, emphasising the man-made, cultural arbitrariness of the 'twenty-four' hours into which the day is divided.

In *The Waves*, it is Louis, the would-be master and maker of global order, whose time is exactly that of the mechanical clock:

> I have fused my many lives into one; I have helped by my assiduity and decision to score those lines on the map there by which the different parts of the world are laced together. I love punctually at ten to come into my room; . . . I love the telephone with its lip stretched to my whisper, and the date on the wall; and the engagement book. Mr Prentice at four; Mr Eyres at four-thirty.[13]

Louis's time is not dominant in *The Waves*, but placed in relation to those of the five other 'characters'. He stands at the most 'civilised' point of a polarity whose other extreme is represented in the 'natural' time of Susan, the mother and country-dweller.

In *Mrs Dalloway*, the imperial Big Ben time is undermined not only by the discontinuous temporalities of the various characters and the double time which they live, but more literally by the belated chiming of other clocks which challenge or mock the precision of Big Ben's time-keeping. The clock with a feminine name follows after:

> Ah, said St Margaret's, like a hostess who comes into her drawing-room on the very stroke of the hour and finds her guests there already. I am not late. No, it is precisely half-past eleven, she says. Yet, though she is perfectly right, her voice, being the voice of the hostess, is reluctant to inflict its individuality. Some grief for the past holds it back; some concern for the present. It is half-past eleven, she says, and the sound of St Margaret's glides into the recesses of the heart and buries itself in ring after ring of sound, like something alive which wants to confide itself, to disperse itself, to be, with a tremor of delight, at rest – like Clarissa herself, thought Peter Walsh, coming downstairs on the stroke of the hour in white.
>
> (*Mrs Dalloway*, p. 54)

Via Peter's thoughts, the narrative makes the already suggested link with the 'hostess' Clarissa explicit, and adds to the connections of that term in Woolf's writing. In 'Mr Bennett and Mrs Brown', the novels of Bennett, Galsworthy and Wells were criticised for their resemblance to hostesses who never get beyond polite introductions to substantive communication. Here, on the other hand, the formalities of the doorstep are not so much prolonged as superfluous in the face of an apparent breach of convention, the guests being already installed. St Margaret's makes of the perfect hostess (there on the dot, and 'perfectly' right) the possibly less than perfect, denying what may be her tardiness. She loses in any case by the fact of asserting and acting on her different view: even if (according to the arbitration of some ultimate clock in the sky) it is actually she who is right, she has *de facto* renounced her status by failing to defer to her guests. So the feminine hostess cannot win: if perfect she is too perfect, merely polite; if other than polite, differing from her guests, she is imperfect.

In contrast to the 'indifference' of Big Ben, St Margaret's wants to connect. Neither wholly neutral nor wholly in the present, 'some grief for the past holds it back; some concern for the present'. It is 'like something alive which wants to confide itself, to disperse itself'. The syntax of this part of the sentence creates a gap between 'to be' and 'at rest', before 'Clarissa herself' appears, and invokes all the uncertainty of her own attitude to life: at once an active pursuit, in the creative 'gift' of her parties, and a retreat into her attic room, a wish like Septimus' to be finally at rest.

Such equivocations on the part of Clarissa/St Margaret's also render questionable her relation to the preceding peal of Big Ben. St Margaret's more doubtful ring could be seen as either complementary (the trivial following the serious, both making a well-tuned ensemble), or lightly mocking (the second bell sounding a gentle mimic), or challenging, by disrupting and detracting from his univocal, authoritative announcement.

The significance of the hostess as clock is thus far from single in its resonances. 'Clarissa herself' epitomises the hostess/woman who barely, but just, finds a harmonious place within the sound and purview of recognised social forms. Whereas Septimus Smith is the extreme 'case' of someone who has lost all contact with the external, common orders of daily life and daily time, Clarissa is questionably situated like St Margaret's, neither within nor without, somewhere between utter differing and absolute conformity. She is close enough to sound or seem as if she simply echoes established authority, and distant enough for her chimes to verge on an expression of doubt or an ironic doubling.

Clarissa is both perfectly conventional in her role as lady and hostess and, at the same time, a misfit: *Mrs Dalloway* is all about the fact that she is still unresolved in a choice apparently completed a generation before. The calm security which is itself the conventional appearance of the hostess is undermined in so far as Clarissa is frequently in different times and places, remaking and reinforcing her preference for Richard over Peter, now structured as a clear-cut opposition between stability and adventure. Like Mrs Ramsay, to all appearances a model of maternal equilibrium, she is in reality anything but 'composed', except in the sense of being put together from disparate parts: 'she always had the feeling that it was very, very dangerous to live even one day' (*Mrs Dalloway*, p. 9).

* * *

[In a passage omitted here Bowlby contrasts *Mrs Dalloway*'s portrayal of individual identity as a 'path' chosen from among other possibilities which still exist as present fantasies, with *The Waves*'s arrangement of six separate but single and consistent lives; and indicates that Mrs Dalloway's own unstable identity is echoed in other characters in the same novel, including the Prime Minister at her party, Hugh Whitbread, Peter Walsh, the 'exiles' Miss Kilman, Rezia, and Maisie Johnson, and even Lady Bruton. Ed.]

Clarissa Dalloway's predicament returns as a question for her daughter. In the same way that, as Elizabeth Abel points out, the significant and unconcluded episode of Clarissa's youth appears to begin and end in late adolescence rather than infancy, Elizabeth Dalloway is a young woman without a past and with many possible future directions: 'Buses swooped, settled, were off – garish caravans, glistening with red and yellow varnish. But which should she get on to? She had no preferences' (p. 148). Unlike her mother's period of hesitation at Bourton, Elizabeth's takes place in the city which can then figure forth the new urban opportunities not available to her mother's generation of women. But Elizabeth's fantasies are represented, as we have seen, as a form of rebellion against maternal wishes; and the narrator, sometimes via the thoughts of the mother, represents her as naïve: 'So she might be a doctor. She might be a farmer. Animals are often ill. She might own a thousand acres and have people under her. She would go and see them in their cottages' (p. 149). This suggests that Elizabeth's professional ideas are childish rather than mature fantasies, and adds force to the hints that she may turn from them to the more usual feminine place she presently refuses: 'For it was beginning. Her mother could see that. The compliments were beginning' (p. 148). Further, the difference between being an object of poetic idealisation and being a professional is structured for Elizabeth as a mutually exclusive opposition of the 'trivial' to the 'serious'. For the time being, she places herself on the masculine side of that valuation, rather than seeking to modify its hierarchy or its terms of exclusion.

Mrs Dalloway makes visible the absence of unity behind the centred façade of 'a woman' deemed to be the emblem of such pacific completion – 'the perfect hostess', married for thirty years – and this then seems to pave the way for the unavoidable non-finality of any course that the daughter may come to take. The indeterminate places of both mother and daughter draw attention to the greater complexity of women's unroyal roads to a femininity that is always other than fully integrated; but also to a greater openness from their very lack of fit with the dominant masculine order. In the fictional '1923', Elizabeth like her mother is still subject to 'some call' upon her to live up to 'the compliments', and the city career she dreams of is marked as a 'serious' escape from a feminine triviality she rejects. It is because and not in spite of this stark division that her 'pioneer' venture into parts of London where Dalloways fear to tread ('For no Dalloways came down the Strand daily' [p. 151]) may lead to the discovery of an identity which is formed otherwise than by the difference between the serious 'procession' of urban conformity and the angel or hostess in the house.

From Rachel Bowlby, *Virginia Woolf, Feminist Destinations* (Oxford, 1988), pp. 80–98.

NOTES

[Rachel Bowlby's book from which this chapter is taken is an exploration of Woolf's changing and unconcluded investigations, in her novels and major essays, of issues of feminism: of what women are and what they might hope to be and do. It precedes its discussion of *Mrs Dalloway* with a chapter on *To the Lighthouse*, seeing that novel as an exploration of ways in which feminine subjectivities conflict with the organised and linear thinking of masculinity, so that both are untenable. Mr Ramsay, and to an extent the other men in the novel, are seen as journeying towards specific goals – the letter R, the lighthouse – and Mrs Ramsay as providing for them both the mother-figure they look back to and a scapegoat for their failures. But she, and Lily, are unable to fit or sustain these roles, so that they threaten the masculine identity that constructs them. Even the different 'temporalities' of the novel's three sections enact the dualism of these systems – the linear and the associative – that depend on but also undermine each other. Bowlby then moves on to discuss *Mrs Dalloway* as an investigation of how to represent 'a more complex feminine or feminist temporality' (p. 79).

In explaining this idea in the essay printed here, Bowlby explores *Mrs Dalloway* in a variety of different critical discourses. She compares Elizabeth and Clarissa and Miss Kilman as realistic representations of the uncertain roles available to women in the London of the 1920s. She compares Woolf's Elizabeth with Jane Eyre and Lucy Snowe, young women confronting life in Charlotte Brontë's novels, and she does this in the context of Virginia Woolf's own ambivalent discussion of *Jane Eyre* in *A Room of One's Own*. She also disputes Elizabeth Abel's psychoanalytic reading (see pp. 147–8 above) that sees Clarissa as having had to abandon her own feminine sexuality to conform to heterosexual marriage, and proposes instead a different reading that sees Clarissa as a fluid feminine consciousness.

As throughout this volume, references to *Mrs Dalloway* are to the Penguin edition with an Introduction and Notes by Elaine Showalter and text edited by Stella McNichol (London, 1992). Ed.]

1. Virginia Woolf, *Three Guineas* (London and New York, 1938; Penguin edition 1977), p. 117.

2. Michèle Barrett (ed.), *Virginia Woolf, Women and Writing* (London and New York, 1979), pp. 57–63. [See my note 3 to Homans's essay, p. 139 above. Ed.]

3. Virginia Woolf, *A Room of One's Own* (London and New York, 1929; Penguin edition 1945, 1992), p. 70.

4. Charlotte Brontë, *Jane Eyre* (1847; Harmondsworth, 1984), p. 140.

5. Ibid., pp. 140–1.

6. Charlotte Brontë, *Villette* (1853; Harmondsworth, 1981), p. 109.

7. Ibid., pp. 117–18.

8. Ibid., p. 107.

9. Difference of class rather than community of sex seems to come to the fore in Woolf's portrayals of 'Unfortunate Julia! wetting her pen in bitterness, and leaving her shoe laces untied' (*Jacob's Room* [London, 1922; Granada edition 1976], p. 103), and (through Katherine Hilberry's eyes) of the odd enthusiasts in the office of a feminist organisation (*Night and Day* [London, 1919; Granada edition 1977], pp. 74–82). And this is perhaps the place to mention also the awkwardness of Woolf's occasional refusal of a relationship between literature and politics, giving support to the myth of Bloomsbury elitism. In 'Mr Bennett and Mrs Brown', for instance, one of the objections to the Edwardians is what she perceives as an imperative to action in their novels: 'In order to complete them it seems necessary to do something – to join a society or, more desperately, to write a cheque. . . . [The Edwardians] were interested in something outside. Their books, then,

were incomplete as books, and required that the reader should finish them, actively and practically, for himself' (Andrew McNeillie (ed.), *The Essays of Virginia Woolf*, vol. 3, *1921–24* [London, 1988], pp. 427–8).

10. Elizabeth Abel, 'Narrative Structure(s) and Female Development: The Case of *Mrs Dalloway*', in Elizabeth Abel, Marianne Hirsch and Elizabeth Langland (eds), *The Voyage In: Fictions of Female Development* (Hanover and London, 1983), p. 171.

11. The Peter Walsh/Richard Dalloway difference may be compared with Woolf's story in *A Sketch of the Past* of the habitual family marking of the difference between her mother's two husbands, 'her two incongruous choices' (Virginia Woolf, *Moments of Being. Unpublished Autobiographical Writings*, ed. Jeanne Schulkind [London, 1976; 1978], p. 105). The first, Herbert Duckworth, figured as the legendary Greek hero; in relation to him, 'the gaunt bearded man' (*Moments of Being*, p. 105), Leslie Stephen, was 'in every way the opposite' (*Moments of Being*, p. 106).

12. Paul Ricoeur, *Temps et récit*, vol. 2, *La Configuration dans le récit de fiction* (ch. 4, n. 8), especially pp. 158–9.

13. Virginia Woolf, *The Waves* (London and New York, 1931; Penguin edition, 1992), pp. 127–8.

Further Reading

EDITIONS

Virginia Woolf's novels, and her other writing published in her lifetime, came out of copyright in Britain in 1991. Various new editions are now being produced. Like many of her novels, *Mrs Dalloway* and *To the Lighthouse* were published simultaneously in London and New York, by the Hogarth Press and Harcourt Brace respectively. Virginia Woolf corrected the proofs for the British and American editions differently, and so British and American readers are familiar with texts that differ from each other in some details.

New editions published in 1991 and 1992 by the Hogarth Press, by Penguin, and by Oxford University Press in the World's Classics Series, are based on the British texts, with major American variants listed. The Shakespeare Head Press Edition, published by Blackwell, is being prepared from collations of the British and American texts. The Shakespeare Head edition of *To the Lighthouse*, edited by Susan Dick and published in 1992, contains a long section of 'Time Passes' which was deleted by Woolf from all proofs of the novel.

The page numbers given for quotations and references to the texts of *Mrs Dalloway* and *To the Lighthouse* in this book have been standardised for convenience. In only one case (see p. 132 above) is there a variation between the text quoted by an American critic and the original British text. References are to:

Virginia Woolf, *Mrs Dalloway*, with an Introduction and Notes by Elaine Showalter and text edited by Stella McNichol (London: Penguin, 1992);
Virginia Woolf, *To the Lighthouse*, with Introduction and Notes by Hermione Lee and text edited by Stella McNichol (London: Penguin, 1992).

These editions are recommended to students. So are:

Virginia Woolf, *Mrs Dalloway*, edited with an Introduction by Claire Tomalin (Oxford: Oxford University Press, 1992);

Virginia Woolf, *To the Lighthouse*, edited with an Introduction by Margaret Drabble (Oxford: Oxford University Press, 1992).

SOME OTHER COLLECTIONS OF ESSAYS

Morris Beja (ed.), *Virginia Woolf, To the Lighthouse*, Casebook (London: Macmillan, 1970). Now old-fashioned examples of readings that saw the novel as mainly 'symbolic'.

Harold Bloom (ed.), *Virginia Woolf's To the Lighthouse* (New York: Chelsea House, 1988). Eight varied and detailed readings.

Rachel Bowlby (ed.), *Virginia Woolf*, Longman Critical Readers Series (Harlow, Essex, and New York: Longman, 1992). A new collection of essays on various aspects of Woolf.

Patricia Clements and Isobel Grundy (eds), *Virginia Woolf: New Critical Essays* (London and Totowa, NJ: Vision, and Barnes & Noble, 1983). Interesting collection of essays focusing especially on narrative construction in various of Woolf's works, and her contemporary context.

Robin Majumdar and Allen McLaurin (eds), *Virginia Woolf, The Critical Heritage* (London and Boston: Routledge & Kegan Paul, 1975). Early reviews of each of Woolf's major works, showing how she was immediately labelled 'poetic'.

Jane Marcus (ed.), *New Feminist Essays on Virginia Woolf* (London: Macmillan, 1981).

Jane Marcus (ed.), *Virginia Woolf and Bloomsbury. A Centenary Celebration* (London: Macmillan, 1987).

Two collections of essays relating Woolf's work to her life and times, mainly with a feminist understanding leading to readings that have been rejected by other writers, especially members and friends of Woolf's family. Jane Marcus has also published three collections of her own essays on Woolf.

Eric Warner (ed.), *Virginia Woolf: A Centenary Perspective* (London: Macmillan; New York: St. Martin's Press, 1984). A rather disappointing collection of papers given at a centenary conference.

RECENT FULL-LENGTH STUDIES OF WOOLF'S WORK

This list includes books which are mentioned or in part reprinted in this book, but which contain useful discussions of *both* novels; and three books relating specifically to *To the Lighthouse*.

Elizabeth Abel, *Virginia Woolf and the Fictions of Psychoanalysis* (Chicago and London: University of Chicago Press, 1989). Reads some of Woolf's texts as workings-out of Freudian theories about gender.

Rachel Bowlby, *Virginia Woolf, Feminist Destinations* (New York and Oxford: Basil Blackwell, 1988). Reads Woolf's major works, not in chronological order, as a series of feminist investigations of feminine identity.

Pamela Caughie, *Virginia Woolf and Postmodernism. Literature in Quest and Question of Itself* (Urbana and Chicago: University of Illinois Press, 1991). A detailed examination of Woolf's texts in an attempt to describe her narrative methods and feminist ideas in 'postmodernist' terms.

Stevie Davies, *Virginia Woolf, To the Lighthouse*, Penguin Critical Studies Series (London and New York: Penguin, 1989). Although vague and at times inaccurate about the novel itself, this book suggests a great variety of intertextual readings.

Daniel Ferrer, trans. Geoffrey Bennington and Rachel Bowlby, *Virginia Woolf and the Madness of Language* (London and New York: Routledge, 1990). A remarkable reading relating Woolf's life and fiction by means of detailed narrative study and linguistic criticism.

C. Ruth Miller, *Virginia Woolf: The Frames of Art and Life* (Basingstoke and London: Macmillan, 1988). An account of Woolf's discussions, overt and implied, about the relation of art to life.

Makiko Minow-Pinkney, *Virginia Woolf and the Problem of the Subject* (Brighton: Harvester Wheatsheaf, 1987). Very detailed reading of the major books in terms of Kristevan theory; a good introduction, in its own right, to psychoanalytic criticism.

Suzanne Raitt, *Virginia Woolf's To the Lighthouse*, Critical Studies of Key Texts Series (Hemel Hempstead: Harvester Wheatsheaf, 1990). A detailed reading of *To the Lighthouse* put in the context of recent feminist and film theory, and of earlier critical discussion.

Su Reid, *To the Lighthouse*, Critics Debate Series (London: Macmillan, 1991). A wide-ranging discussion of readings of the novel since its publication, and a brief new reading.

Sue Roe, *Writing and Gender. Virginia Woolf's Writing Practice* (Hemel Hempstead: Harvester Wheatsheaf; New York: St. Martin's Press, 1990). A detailed and stimulating examination of Woolf's changing practice and intentions in her writing.

Alex Zwerdling, *Virginia Woolf and the Real World* (Los Angeles and London: University of California Press, 1986). An interesting account of some of the ways in which Woolf's work reflects social and historical issues.

OTHER ESSAYS ON WOOLF BY CONTRIBUTORS TO THIS VOLUME

Elizabeth Abel, 'Narrative Structure(s) and Female Development: The Case of Mrs Dalloway', in Elizabeth Abel, Marianne Hirsch and Elizabeth Langland (eds), *The Voyage In. Fictions of Female Development* (Hanover and London: University Press of New England, 1983), pp. 161–85. An account of *Mrs Dalloway* as an exploration of female silencing.

Gillian Beer, 'Beyond Determinism: George Eliot and Virginia Woolf', in her *Arguing with the Past. Essays in Narrative from Woolf to Sidney* (London and New York: Routledge, 1989), pp. 117–37. A comparison of reactions to determinist thought in works by Eliot and Woolf, especially *Middlemarch*, *The Mill on the Floss*, *Orlando* and *The Waves*.

Gillian Beer, 'The Victorians in Virginia Woolf: 1832–1941', *Arguing with the Past*, pp. 138–58. An account of a reminiscence of Victorianism, and an awareness of its end, in most of Woolf's novels.

Gillian Beer, 'Virginia Woolf and Prehistory', *Arguing with the Past*, pp. 159–82. An account of references to the prehistoric, and particularly to

Darwinian and post-Darwinian thinking about prehistory, particularly in *The Voyage Out* and *Between the Acts*.

Gillian Beer, 'The Body of the People in Virginia Woolf', in Sue Roe (ed.), *Women Reading Women's Writing* (Brighton: Harvester Press, 1987), pp. 85–114. A wide study of communities of people – families, friends, nations – in Woolf's writings.

Gillian Beer, 'The Island and the Aeroplane: the Case of Virginia Woolf', in Homi K. Bhabha (ed.), *Nation and Narration* (London and New York: Routledge, 1990), pp. 265–90. Accounts of aeroplanes in Woolf's *Diary* and novels, and their implications about changing ideas of nationhood.

Rachel Bowlby, 'Walking, Women and Writing: Virginia Woolf as Flâneuse', in Isobel Armstrong (ed.), *New Feminist Discourses. Critical Essays on Theories and Texts* (London and New York: Routledge, 1992), pp. 26–47; included in Rachel Bowlby, *Still Crazy After All These Years. Women, Writing, and Psychoanalysis* (London and New York: Routledge, 1993). A debate about Woolf and writing about walking, and the transformation of women in writing from the role of passer-by.

Rachel Bowlby, 'A More Than Maternal Tie'; Introduction to Virginia Woolf, *A Woman's Essays*, ed. Rachel Bowlby (London and New York: Penguin, 1992), pp. ix–xxxiii. A comparative survey of ideas about women and writing in Woolf's essays. This volume of Woolf's essays is to be followed by another, *The Crowded Dance of Modern Life*.

John Mepham, 'Mourning and Modernism', in Patricia Clements and Isobel Grundy (eds), *Virginia Woolf: New Critical Essays* (London and Totowa, NJ: Vision, and Barnes & Noble, 1983), pp. 137–56. An account of the narration of *Mrs Dalloway* as a rejection of an authoritative voice.

J. Hillis Miller, 'Between the Acts: Repetition as Extrapolation', in his *Fiction and Repetition. Seven English Novels* (Cambridge, Mass: Harvard University Press; Oxford: Basil Blackwell: 1982), pp. 203–31.

J. Hillis Miller, 'Mr Carmichael and Lily Briscoe: The Rhythm of Creativity in *To the Lighthouse*', in Robert Kiely and John Hildebidle (eds), *Modernism Reconsidered* (Cambridge, Mass., and London: Harvard University Press, 1983), pp. 167–89.

The two essays above continue the account in Miller's essay on *Mrs Dalloway*, partly reprinted in this volume, of how meanings are created in the reading of Woolf.

Makiko Minow-Pinkney, 'Virginia Woolf: Seen From a Foreign Land', in John Fletcher and Andrew Benjamin (eds), *Abjection, Melancholia, and Love. The Work of Julia Kristeva* (London and New York: Routledge, 1990), pp. 157–77. A further Kristevan study, especially of *The Waves*.

SOME EARLIER, AND OTHER, FULL-LENGTH CRITICAL ACCOUNTS OF WOOLF

Nancy Topping Bazin, *Virginia Woolf and the Androgynous Vision* (New Brunswick, NJ: Rutgers University Press, 1973).

Maria DiBattista, *Virginia Woolf's Major Novels: The Fables of Anon* (New Haven, Conn., and London: Yale University Press, 1980).

Ralph Freedman, *Virginia Woolf: Revaluation and Continuity* (Berkeley: University of California Press, 1980).
Jean Guiget, *Virginia Woolf and her Works*, trans. Jean Stewart (New York: Harcourt, Brace & World, 1965).
Hermione Lee, *The Novels of Virginia Woolf* (London: Methuen, 1977).
Herbert Marder, *Feminism and Art. A Study of Virginia Woolf* (Chicago and London: University of Chicago Press, 1968).
Allen McLaurin, *Virginia Woolf, The Echoes Enslaved* (Cambridge and New York: Cambridge University Press, 1973).
James Naremore, *The World Without a Self. Virginia Woolf and the Novel* (New Haven and London: Yale University Press, 1973).
Michael Rosenthal, *Virginia Woolf* (London and Henley: Routledge & Kegan Paul, 1979).

BIOGRAPHIES OF WOOLF

The last two decades have produced many conflicting versions of Woolf's story. This is a selection.

Quentin Bell, *Virginia Woolf. A Biography*, 2 vols (London: Hogarth Press; New York: Harcourt Brace Jovanovich, 1972). Written by Woolf's nephew using family papers, and very detailed. Its accounts of Woolf's 'madness' have been challenged by subsequent writers.
Louise DeSalvo, *Virginia Woolf: The Impact of Childhood Sexual Abuse on Her Life and Work* (Boston: Beacon Press; London, Women's Press, 1989). Highly publicised reading of Woolf's life and works.
Lyndall Gordon, *Virginia Woolf. A Writer's Life* (Oxford and London: Oxford University Press; New York: W. W. Norton, 1984). A detailed and balanced account using Woolf's own writings, including recently published autobiographical material.
John Mepham, *Virginia Woolf. A Literary Life* (Basingstoke and London: Macmillan, 1991). A careful account, relating the writing to Woolf's life.
Roger Poole, *The Unknown Virginia Woolf* (Cambridge: Cambridge University Press, 1978). A careful reconstruction of Woolf's life largely from her own writings, including her novels.
Phyllis Rose, *Woman of Letters. A Life of Virginia Woolf* (New York: Oxford University Press, 1978; revised edition London: Pandora Press, 1986). A feminist interpretation, disagreeing with Bell and using readings of the novels.

SOME USEFUL INTRODUCTIONS TO RECENT CRITICAL THEORY

Mary Eagleton (ed.), *Feminist Literary Criticism*, Longman Critical Readers Series (Harlow and New York: Longman, 1991). An excellent anthology of important essays.
Terry Eagleton (ed.), *Literary Theory. An Introduction* (Oxford: Blackwell, 1983). The most popular review of literary theory and the changes in 'English' over a decade.
Roger Fowler, *Linguistic Criticism* (Oxford and New York: Oxford Univer-

sity Press, 1986). An accessible introduction to the linguistic study of literature, especially narratives.

David Lodge (ed.), *Modern Criticism and Theory. A Reader* (London and New York: Longman, 1988). Very wide selection of indicative essays.

Toril Moi, *Sexual/Textual Politics: Feminist Literary Theory* (London and New York: Methuen, 1985). Very influential introduction to French feminist theory, especially favouring Julia Kristeva.

Christopher Norris, *Deconstruction: Theory and Practice* (London and New York: Methuen, 1982). An account of the origins and developments of Derridean criticism.

Raman Selden, *Practising Theory and Reading Literature. An Introduction* (London and New York: Harvester Wheatsheaf, 1989). A clear and helpful overview.

Robyn R. Warhol and Diane Price Herndl (eds), *Feminisms. An Anthology of Literary Theory and Criticism* (New Brunswick, NJ: Rutgers University Press, 1991). An excellent American anthology of feminist criticism and critical theory.

Chris Weedon, *Feminist Practice and Poststructuralist Theory* (Oxford and New York: Blackwell, 1987). A clear account of theories of gender and their application in critical practice.

Notes on Contributors

Elizabeth Abel is Associate Professor of English at the University of California at Berkeley. She edited *Writing and Sexual Difference* (1982), an important collection of American essays in feminist criticism, and with others, *The Voyage In. Fictions of Female Development* (1983) and *The Signs Reader: Women, Gender and the Scholarship* (1983). She has more recently published *Virginia Woolf and the Fictions of Psychoanalysis* (1989).

Gillian Beer is Professor of English in the University of Cambridge and a Fellow of Girton College. Her recent books include *Darwin's Plots* (1983), *George Eliot* (1986), and *Arguing with the Past. Essays in Narrative from Woolf to Sidney* (1989).

Rachel Bowlby is Reader in English at the University of Sussex. She is the author of numerous articles, and of *Just Looking. Consumer Culture in Dreiser, Gissing, and Zola* (1985), *Virginia Woolf, Feminist Destinations* (1988), and *Still Crazy After All These Years. Women, Writing, and Psychoanalysis* (1993). She edited *Virginia Woolf: A Woman's Essays* (1992) and, with Geoffrey Bennington, has translated Daniel Ferrer, *Virginia Woolf and the Madness of Language* (1990).

Margaret Homans is Professor of English at Yale University. She has written *Women Writers and Poetic Identity* (1980) as well as *Bearing the Word* (1986), and is working on a book about contemporary African American writers.

David Lodge was Professor of Modern English Literature at Birmingham University until 1987, since when he has been a full-time writer. He has made a major contribution to the study of prose fiction and of literary theory in Britain: in addition to *The Modes of Modern Writing* his critical works include *Language of Fiction* (1966), *The Novelist at the Crossroads* (1971), *Working with Structuralism* (1981), *Write On* (1986), and *After Bakhtin. Essays on Fiction and Criticism* (1990), and he has edited two anthologies of essays in critical theory, *Twentieth Century Literary Criticism* (1972) and *Modern Criticism and Theory* (1988). Some of his thinking about literature, criticism, religious and philosophical issues, and about Higher Education, has reached a wider audience in his comic novels of which the most recent are *Changing Places* (1975), *How Far Can You Go?* (1980), *Small World* (1984), *Nice Work* (1988) and *Paradise News* (1991).

John Mepham studied biochemistry and the history and philosophy of science, before teaching both English and philosophy at the University of Sussex and then becoming a freelance writer. He has written and translated works of philosophy and critical theory and edited the four-volume *Issues in Marxist Philosophy* (1979–84) with David-Hillel Ruben. Recently he has written study guides to *Mrs Dalloway* (1986) and *To the Lighthouse* (1987), and *Virginia Woolf, A Literary Life* (1991).

J. Hillis Miller is Distinguished Professor of English and Comparative Literature at the University of California at Irvine. His most recent books are *The Linguistic Moment: From Wordsworth to Stevens* (1987), *The Ethics of Reading* (1987), *Versions of Pygmalion* (1990), and *Hawthorne and History* (1990), as well as three volumes of collected essays: *Victorian Subjects* (1990), *Tropes, Parables, Performatives* (1990), and *Theory Now and Then* (1991).

Makiko Minow-Pinkney is author of *Virginia Woolf and the Problem of the Subject* (1987), and of a forthcoming study of Julia Kristeva. She is a member of the editorial board of *News from Nowhere* and has recently been teaching at the University of Lancaster.

Toril Moi is Professor of Literature at Duke University and Adjunct Professor of Comparative Literature at the University of Bergen. She is the author of *Sexual/Textual Politics: Feminist Literary Theory* (1985), and *Feminist Theory and Simone de Beauvoir* (1990), and the editor of *The Kristeva Reader* (1986) and *French Feminist Thought* (1987).

Jeremy Tambling teaches in the Department of Comparative Literature at the University of Hong Kong. He is the author of *Opera, Ideology and Film* (1987), *Dante and Difference: Writing in the 'Commedia'* (1988), *What is Literary Language?* (1988), *Confession: Sin, Sexuality and the Subject* (1990), and *Narrative and Ideology* (1991).

Index